7 Days of Prayer

Daily Services of Private Worship

Compiled by

Stephen Phifer

Copyright © 2024 by Stephen Phifer

All rights reserved. No part of this publication may be reproduced, distributed, or transmitted in any form or by any means, including photocopying, recording, or other electronic or mechanical methods, without the prior written permission of the publisher, except in the case of brief quotations embodied in critical reviews and certain other noncommercial uses permitted by copyright law. For permission requests, write to the publisher at publishing@kingdomwinds.com.

Scripture quotations marked *(NIV)* are taken from the Holy Bible, New International Version®, NIV®. Copyright © 1973, 1978, 1984, 2011 by Biblica, Inc.® Used by permission of Zondervan. All rights reserved worldwide. www.zondervan.com The *"NIV"* and *"New International Version"* are trademarks registered in the United States Patent and Trademark Office by Biblica, Inc.®

Scripture quotations marked *(NKJV)* are taken from the New King James Version®. Copyright © 1982 by Thomas Nelson. Used by permission. All rights reserved.

Scripture quotations marked *(ESV)* are taken from the ESV® Bible *(The Holy Bible, English Standard Version®)*. ESV® Text Edition: 2016. Copyright © 2001 by Crossway, a publishing ministry of Good News Publishers. The ESV® text has been reproduced in cooperation with and by permission of Good News Publishers. Unauthorized reproduction of this publication is prohibited. All rights reserved.

Scripture quotations marked *(NLT)* are taken from the Holy Bible, New Living Translation, copyright © 1996, 2004, 2015 by Tyndale House Foundation. Used by permission of Tyndale House Publishers, Inc., Carol Stream, Illinois 60188. All rights reserved.

First Edition, 2024.

ISBN 13: 978-1-64590-057-3

Published by Kingdom Winds Publishing.
www.kingdomwinds.com
publishing@kingdomwinds.com
Printed in the United States of America.
The views expressed in this book are not necessarily those of the publisher.

Dedication

This contemporary prayer book is dedicated to the prayer warriors in my family: my father and mother, J.D. and Ruth Phifer, my brother, the late Dr. James D. Phifer, my daughters and their husbands, Matt and Nicole Huett, and Manny and Jennifer Foret, my wife Freeda whose prayers are mighty through God to the pulling down of strongholds, and her parents, Mr. and Mrs. B. B. Woolf.

Also, this book is dedicated to my friend Dr. James Hart, former president of the Robert E. Webber Institute for Worship Studies. Jim was my faculty advisor for my doctoral thesis, *Experiment in Prayer*, in which the first version of this prayer book appeared.

Contents

The Call to Pray 7

Instructions for Use 13

Sunday 19

Monday 29

Tuesday 41

Wednesday 53

Thursday 65

Friday 77

Saturday 89

Evening Prayer 101

Dr. Stephen Phifer 110

INTRODUCTION

The Call to Pray

EXCERPT FROM *Into the Secret Place (2021)*

The call of God comes to us in spiritual sounds, inaudible to the human ear, but insistent deep in the human heart. We hear this call when we stare at that horizon where the sea and sky dance together in the wind. It comes to us clearly when we ascend some precipice of note to gaze at distant lands shrouded in mist. In the quiet of the late-night hours, we hear it in our dreams or in those sleepless times when our minds will not be still. We sense the call in the fellowship of those we love and trust, in moments so soon to pass, and never to be relived.

In biblical terms, this is a witness born deep in our flawed human spirit, a connection with the Holy Spirit of God. It is a deep conviction that we belong to Him, though we are separated from Him. Hear the words of the Apostle Paul:

> *Therefore, brethren, we are debtors—not to the flesh, to live according to the flesh. For if you live according to the flesh you will die; but if by the Spirit you put to death the deeds of the body, you will live. For as many as are led by the Spirit of God, these are sons of God. For you did not receive the spirit of bondage again to fear, but you received the Spirit of adoption by whom we cry out, "Abba, Father." The Spirit Himself bears witness with our spirit that we are children of God, and if children, then heirs—heirs of God and joint heirs with Christ, if indeed we suffer with Him, that we may also be glorified together. (Romans 8:12–17, NKJV)*

"*His Spirit bears witness with our spirit.*" This is the call to pray. For those without a biblical worldview, this call can lead them to all sorts of misguided pursuits. These are born in the soul—the mind and heart where ideas and feelings boil together in the heat of circumstance—but they are executed in the body to momentary pleasure and eventual pain. Many believe the lie that there is no spirit within them, no capacity to know God, and no destiny beyond the here and now. Others resist such foolishness with spiritualities born of cultural lies presenting false gods and fruitless hopes, wasting their spiritual energy in post-modern paganism.

There is a better way, a way born in ancient truth, proven by experience and by the close presence of the Divine, the God of Abraham, Isaac, and Jacob, the Jehovah of Old Testament saints, the Heavenly Father of New Testament disciples, the Risen Christ of our historical church fathers, the Living Word of the Reformers, and The Faithful God of our own parents.

For us, too, there is a way to clearly hear the call and to answer it. This call is the deep desire to have an on-going fellowship with our Maker. It is true that sin has separated us from God, but God has always had a plan. In the Old Covenant, sin demanded a thick curtain called the veil to stand between a holy God and a sinful humanity. The Gospel of Christ is Good News precisely because this heavy veil was torn from the top to the bottom when Jesus cried, *"It is finished!"* from Calvary's cross[1]. His innocent death paid the price for all our sins, opening to us the *"new and living way"* to hear and answer the call to pray. Hear the words of the Hebrew Correspondent:

> *Therefore, brethren, having boldness to enter the Holiest by the blood of Jesus, by a new and living way which He consecrated for us, through the veil, that is, His flesh, and having a High Priest over the house of God, let us draw near with a true heart in full assurance of faith, having our hearts sprinkled from an evil conscience and our bodies washed with pure water. (Hebrews 10:1922, NKJV)*

Noun and Verb

The Call to Pray involves both the noun, *"prayer,"* and the verb, *"to pray."* We must understand what prayer is, and we must actually pray. For most of us, prayer has been reduced to petitions, a means of asking God for things. This is only a small part of the whole reality of prayer. What is it, then?

---

1 John 19:30, NKJV

Prayer is fellowship with God. In this time of fellowship we read and listen to His Word. We hear His voice in His creation and in the words of others. We wait in His holy presence. We praise Him with our own words and with the ancient words of those who came before us. We worship Him with hearts made clean by His own blood. And we rehearse again and again the revelation of who God is as revealed in Scripture.

Prayer is so much more than petitioning! It takes on many forms and engages our entire human self in these many processes. *Into the Secret Place*, is a careful biblical, historical, and practical exposition of the noun, and is a collection of inspirational essays to encourage you to pray. *7 Days of Prayer* is a set of personal services to aid you as you pray.

Hearing and Obeying the Call

It can accurately be said that life is all about hearing and obeying the call to pray. Before we commit our lives to Jesus, we hear everywhere His call to follow Him. Creation beckons us. If enigmas, the unanswerable questions of life, confuse us, they also point the way to One whose ways are higher than our ways. The peace of those who follow Him astounds and attracts us.

When we become a part of His Kingdom, we hear this call to daily time with the Father. Along the way, as we walk with God, we hear a specific call to the way or ways He has chosen for us to serve Him. Weekly, we hear the call to fellowship with others who are following Him.

At this point, a marvelous thing happens for us. The very truths that we have encountered, confessed, and responded to when we obeyed the call to pray every day are reinforced in the public meeting. In this way, private prayer and public prayer feed each other! We hear and obey the call to pray every day and every week.

An Amazing Promise

Jesus walked this earth as a man who prayed. It is interesting to note that with all the wonderful things Jesus did, His disciples asked Him to teach them to pray. They did not ask that He teach them to heal the sick, or scatter demons, or raise the dead, or turn water to wine, or to walk on water or even to still the storm. They said, *"Lord, teach us to pray."*[2] And He did.

We will take a careful look at the teachings of Jesus on prayer and at the subsequent teaching of the disciples. By way of introduction, one promise needs emphasis here for it lies at the heart of this book. In the Sermon on the Mount, Jesus gave us a prayer to pray and a promise to believe. Hear the words of Jesus:

> *But you, when you pray, go into your room, and when you have shut your door, pray to your Father who is in the secret place; and your Father who sees in secret will reward you openly. (Matthew 6:6, NKJV)*

In these few words, Jesus promises that the power of heaven will impact our everyday lives. Note these important truths:

There is a place to pray called, *"The Secret Place."* This *removes* from us any performance before anyone else—we have a private audience with God!

God the Father is there. Not only does He occupy the Throne of Majesty in the Heavenly Zion, He is there with us in the Secret Place!

The Father is paying attention to us. The book of Revelation indicates that the prayers of the saints are collected in the presence of God in golden bowls.[3] God records and remembers what He sees and hears in the Secret Place of Prayer.

God the Father rewards openly what happens and what is said in the Secret Place.

The Christ-follower who longs for a life that counts here on earth and in eternity must answer the call of Jesus to the Secret Place. Here is where victories are won. This is the place where God becomes known to us. **"This the power station where the might of the Holy Spirit is gained."**

---

2   Luke 11:1, NIV

3   Rev. 5:8

Backstory

Into the Secret Place tells two stories: the biblical and historical story of private prayer and the story of my struggle with private worship. The exposition of the truth about prayer is taken from my doctoral thesis *Experiment in Prayer: The Convergence of Fixed and Extemporaneous Prayers in the Lives of Believers at Word of Life International Church, Springfield, VA*. This work completed the Doctor of Worship Studies degree for me at The Robert E. Webber Institute for Worship Studies in 2004. The *7 Days of Prayer* prayer book is a recent revision of *The Book of Private Worship* I compiled for my thesis. The introductory chapters place this research into my life story, and the concluding chapters continue my story in the years since 2004. Included in this section are inspirational essays from my writing ministry website and selected material from my first book, *Worship that Pleases God: The Passion and Reason of True Worship (Trafford Publishers, 2005)*.

The Story Goes On!

Your story and mine are still being told! God is still calling us to pray, and as we do, we can live lives that are pleasing to the Lord and are of great benefit to those who know us!

— Stephen Phifer

Instructions for Use

To be a Christian is to be a worshiper. Jesus told us the Heavenly Father was looking for true worshipers—those who would worship Him in Spirit and in Truth. The New Testament encourages worshipers to continue to meet together to worship. We are also instructed to pray without ceasing, to continually offer the sacrifice of praise and to offer every activity of life to the Lord as worship. Worship, then, is at the heart of being a Christian.

Worship is personal. We cannot delegate our worship to others. Each believer must actively engage the body, soul, and spirit in worship. Public worship services are planned for us by our worship leaders, so all we have to do is join in with heart, soul, mind, and strength. Where can we find a plan and structure for our personal, private worship? This has been a challenge in every age of Christianity.

It has been a lifelong struggle for me. I was a worship leader who excelled at public worship and struggled with personal, private worship. Every new year brought a new attempt. At age 51, I experienced a breakthrough when I discovered *The Book of Common Prayer*. For the first time, I was able to consistently minister to the Lord as a private worshiper. All those years, I had lacked this: a personal worship service. I needed a private structure similar to the one I provided my congregations. This is exactly what I found in *The Book of Common Prayer* and have compiled in *7 Days of Prayer*.

Apostolic Prayer

In every age of Christianity, when reforms are sought in worship, reformers seek out the principles and practices of the apostles. My conviction is that the apostles prayed in three basic ways:

- **Liturgical prayers** (written prayers),
- **Extemporaneous prayers** (improvised, conversational prayers)
- **Prayer in a spiritual language** (prayer in the Holy Spirit), and this is, I believe, what Paul referred to in his instructions to the church at Ephesus:

    And pray in the Spirit on all occasions with all kinds of prayers and requests. With this in mind, be alert and always keep on praying for all the Lord's people. (Ephesians 6:18, NIV)

7 Days of Prayer is designed to re-establish the full dimension of apostolic prayer. Let the liturgical prayers, Scriptures, and confessions empower your extemporaneous praise, worship, and petition. While prayer in the language of the Spirit resists planning, my experience has been that at any time in these personal services of worship, the Holy Spirit may give me utterance in my prayer language to praise and worship the Lord or to intercede.

Characteristics of 7 Days of Prayer

The Book of Daily Prayer is designed for the 21st-century worshiper. These are the important characteristics:

- **Multiple Sources.** My sources are *The Book of Common Prayer*, Scripture passages, and prayers I have composed. You may wish to add the texts of great hymns and contemporary praise and worship songs at appropriate points.
- **Modern English.** I have avoided Elizabethan pronouns and verbs with the use of modern translations of Scripture.
- **Scripture Reading.** Space is allotted in each service for the reading of Psalms, Old Testament, and New Testament passages of Scriptures

- **Listening Prayer.** After each Bible reading, you may wish to have a time of silent reflection or listening prayer. This keeps the two-way communication of prayer in focus.
- **Personal Prayers.** Space is allotted for you to present your petitions to the Lord.

Structure of 7 Days of Prayer

The prayer book contains two sections:

- **Seven Days of Morning Prayer.** A service is designed for every day of the week. The Monday-Friday prayers are concerned with the workweek, and the Saturday-Sunday prayers are for the weekend. The daily confessions balance Old Covenant and New Covenant expressions of worship. These services also include various intercessions and closing prayers. These are to be used as needed. Morning prayer should be as close to the beginning of the day as possible. Evening prayer can be at nightfall or just before retiring.
- **One Service of Evening Prayer.** This beautiful service is designed for nightfall and can be just as effective at bedtime. Its structure is similar to the morning services, but the emphasis is on prayers for rest and safety through the night and continued confidence in the Lord as the one who never sleeps, keeping watch over those who love Him.

The Monday-Friday services have this structure: Invocation. Call to Worship, Confessions of Praise, Confessions of Worship, Prayers of Repentance, Scriptures for the Day, The Psalms, Old Testament Reading, New Testament Reading, Prayers of Petition, Confessions of Faith, and Benediction.

The Saturday-Sunday services are structured differently.

Repeated Prayers and Prayer Selections

Many prayers are used every day, while some are appointed to certain days. Different Scripture readings each morning and evening add variety.

You may also choose any or all the prayers in the closing prayers section and in the evening service.

Suggestions for Use

Regular Times for Worship
You may adjust the times to match your "**morning-person**" or "**night-person**" temperament.

A Place to Pray
I recommend that your times of morning and evening worship take place in the same locations, preferably ones free of interruptions. This provides a sense of an appointment with the Lord. Carefully construct the atmosphere of your place of prayer to heighten your spirituality. Something about candlelight helps me pray, so I have used a candle stand with three candles that remind me of the Trinity. For morning worship, I have used a chair in our living room. There is a handy table for my Bible and prayer books. Evening worship is scripted to take place at nightfall, so a place where the fading of daylight can be observed during worship is recommended. Here in Florida, I love to sit on a screened-in porch at our home. Of course, the evening service is also meaningful at bedtime. Recently, I have been driving to a lake in a city park as my prayer-place.

Suggested Practices

- **Daily Morning and Evening Prayers.** The seven morning services contain a variety of prayers for each day. The evening prayer service is useful every night. Morning prayers include prayers on a three-day rotation. Closing prayers may be used for either morning or evening services.

- **Once a day.** Prayers of repentance and personal petitions may only be needed once a day. If morning prayer is missed, be sure to include them in the evening prayer.

- **Be careful of background music.** Since contemporary and traditional worship songs are centered upon their texts, words in the background (either sung or implied instrumentally) will divide your mind. If you need music, I recommend Baroque, Classical, Early Romantic instrumental music, or some other music without word association. Silence or the sounds of nature are the recommended backgrounds.

- **Read aloud.** These prayers, whether from Scripture, tradition, or from old or new songs, are intended to be read aloud. *"Faith comes by hearing,"* the Bible says in Romans. While I have found these services to be effective, when I could not read aloud, on an airplane for instance, their power increases with the act of reading aloud, even if it is only a whisper.

- **Keep your focus.** Avoid distractions. Personal worship is all about loving God with heart, soul, mind, and strength. Ask family members to help protect your time and space for daily worship. Keep a note pad handy to write down work, family, or other concerns that come into your mind during prayer. This way, you will not forget them, and they are dismissed in as short a time as possible. Things that need prayer can be added to your extemporaneous prayer when you reach that point in the service.

- **Compose your own prayers.** When it is time in the service to present your personal petitions to the Lord, you may want to pray for needs as they come to mind. You may want to compile a prayer list to aid extemporaneous prayer. You may also want to compose prayers based on those in the service for each of the people and needs on your list. If you are struggling with a certain issue, a daily prayer composed for that need can really be used by the Lord in your life.

I trust that your relationship with the Lord Jesus will be enriched by these services of Daily Prayer.

Dr. Stephen Phifer

7 DAYS OF PRAYER

Sunday

Invocation

Before Worship

BCP[1], *adaptation mine*[2]
O Almighty God, who pours out on all who desire it the spirit of grace and of supplication: Deliver me as I draw near to You, from coldness of heart and wanderings of mind, that with steadfast thoughts and kindled affections I may worship You in spirit and in truth; through Jesus Christ our Lord. *Amen.*

Psalm 43:3, **BCP**[3]
Send out Your light and Your truth, that they may lead me, and bring me to Your holy hill and to Your dwelling.

Call to Worship

Psalm 122:1, **BCP**

---

1 BCP is the abbreviation for the Book of Common Prayer

2 All references to BCP for the purposes of this prayer book are taken from *The Book of Common Prayer, Oxford University Press*, USA 2000. Text adapted where noted.

3 *The Book of Common Prayer* includes a translation of the Book of Psalms.

I was glad when they said to me, *"Let us go to the house of the Lord."* (BCP)

***Habakkuk 2:20*, NIV**
The Lord is in his holy temple; let all the earth be silent before him.

In a short season of silence, draw away from the world and draw near to the Lord Jesus.

Confessions of Praise

***Psalm 99:5;9*, NIV**
Exalt the LORD our God and worship at his footstool; he is holy. Exalt the LORD our God and worship at his holy mountain, for the LORD our God is holy.

***Psalm 24:7–10*, NIV**
Lift up your heads, you gates; be lifted up, you ancient doors, that the King of glory may come in. Who is this King of glory? The LORD strong and mighty, the LORD mighty in battle. Lift up your heads, you gates; lift them up, you ancient doors, that the King of glory may come in. Who is he, this King of glory? The LORD Almighty—he is the King of glory.

***Psalm 100*, NIV**
Shout for joy to the LORD, all the earth. Worship the LORD with gladness; come before him with joyful songs. Know that the LORD is God. It is he who made us, and we are his; we are his people, the sheep of his pasture. Enter his gates with thanksgiving and his courts with praise; give thanks to him and praise his name. For the LORD is good and his love endures forever; his faithfulness continues through all generations.

***Psalm 150*, NKJV**
Praise the LORD! Praise God in His sanctuary; Praise Him in His mighty firmament! Praise Him for His mighty acts; Praise Him according to His excellent greatness! Praise Him with the sound of the trumpet; Praise Him with the lute and harp! Praise Him with the timbrel and dance; Praise Him with stringed instruments and flutes! Praise Him with loud cymbals; Praise Him with clashing cymbals! Let everything that has breath praise the LORD. Praise the LORD!

Psalm 145:3–7, **NIV**
Great is the LORD and most worthy of praise; his greatness no one can fathom. One generation commends your works to another; they tell of your mighty acts. They speak of the glorious splendor of your majesty—and I will meditate on your wonderful works. They tell of the power of your awesome works, and I will proclaim your great deeds. They celebrate your abundant goodness and joyfully sing of your righteousness.

Confessions of Worship

Psalm 22:3–5, **NKJV**
… You are holy, Enthroned in the praises of Israel. Our fathers trusted in You; They trusted, and You delivered them. They cried to You, and were delivered; They trusted in You, and were not ashamed.

Psalm 32:7, **NKJV**
You are my hiding place; You shall preserve me from trouble; You shall surround me with songs of deliverance.

Psalm 86:5, **NKJV**
For You, Lord, are good, and ready to forgive, And abundant in mercy to all those who call upon You.

Psalm 97:9, **NKJV**
For You, LORD, are most high above all the earth; You are exalted far above all gods.

Psalm 118:28–29, **NKJV**
You are my God, and I will praise You; You are my God, I will exalt You. Oh, give thanks to the LORD, for He is good! For His mercy endures forever.

Prayers of Repentance

BCP *(adaptation mine)*
Most merciful God, I confess that I have sinned against You in thought, word, and deed, by what I have done, and by what I have left undone. I

have not loved You with my whole heart; I have not loved my neighbor as myself. I am truly sorry, and I humbly repent. For the sake of Your Son, Jesus Christ, have mercy on me and forgive me; that I may delight in Your will and walk in Your ways, to the glory of your Name. *Amen.*

Almighty God has mercy on me. He forgives me all my sins through our Lord Jesus Christ. He strengthens me in all goodness, and by the power of the Holy Spirit keeps me in eternal life. *Amen.*

Scriptures for the Day

BCP *(adaptation mine)*
Lord, open my lips. And my mouth shall proclaim Your praise.

Glory to the Father, and to the Son, and to the Holy Spirit: As it was in the beginning, is now, and will be forever. *Amen.*

The Psalms

Prayerfully read Psalms selected for the day or in sequence.

(At the end of the Psalms)
Glory to the Father, and to the Son, and to the Holy Spirit: As it was in the beginning, is now, and will be forever. *Amen.*

During a time of silence and listening prayer, reflect on the passages you have read.

Old Testament Reading

Systemically read passages from Old Testament books.

(Before the Reading)
Hope in the Word
Psalm 119:73–74, NIV

Your hands made me and formed me; give me understanding to learn Your commands. May those who fear you rejoice when they see me, for I have put my hope in your word.

(After the Reading)
The Word of the Lord. Thanks be to God.

During a time of silence and listening prayer, reflect on the passages you have read.

New Testament Reading

Systemically read passages from New Testament Books.

(Before the Reading)
Prayer for Spiritual Vision
***Ephesians 1:17-19** (adapted from the NIV)*
O glorious Father, give me the Spirit of wisdom and revelation, so that I may know You better. I pray also that the eyes of my heart may be enlightened in order that I may know the hope to which You have called me, the riches of my glorious inheritance in the saints, and Your incomparably great power for us who believe.

(After the Reading)
The Word of the Lord. Thanks be to God.

During a time of silence and listening prayer, reflect on the passages you have read.

Prayers of Petition

The Lord's Prayer
BCP
Our Father in heaven, hallowed be Your Name, Your kingdom come, Your will be done, on earth as in heaven. Give us today our daily bread. Forgive us our sins as we forgive those who sin against us. Save us from the time of trial and deliver us from evil. For the kingdom, the power, and the glory are Yours, now and forever. *Amen.*

For Sunday
BCP

O God, You make us glad with the weekly remembrance of the glorious resurrection of Your Son our Lord: Give us this day such blessing through our worship of You, that the week to come may be spent in Your favor; through Jesus Christ our Lord. *Amen.*

For the Church
BCP

Gracious Father, we pray for Your holy universal Church. Fill it with all truth, in all truth with all peace. Where it is corrupt, purify it; where it is in error, direct it; where in anything it is amiss, reform it. Where it is right, strengthen it; where it is in want, provide for it; where it is divided, reunite it; for the sake of Jesus Christ thy Son our Savior. *Amen.*

For the Mission of the Church
BCP

Ever-living God, whose will it is that all should come to You through Your Son Jesus Christ: Inspire our witness to Him, that all may know the power of His forgiveness and the hope of His resurrection; who lives and reigns with You and the Holy Spirit, one God, now and forever. *Amen.*

A Prayer for the Sanctuary
SRP[4]

O Sovereign Lord, grant that our Sanctuary would be a place where praises go up and grace comes down, proud hearts are humbled and searching souls are redeemed, broken hearts are mended and shattered minds are renewed.

Let this be the place where The Truth rises on shouts as well as songs, the Glory falls on hungry hearts, the Voice of the Spirit, the Call of God, is heard once more, the Anointing flows in fullness, and The Word of God is proclaimed with authority.

Let this hallowed room be the place where the Holy Spirit rules in power, Jesus, the Savior-Healer-Baptizer, walks among us, and the Loving Heavenly Father embraces the Prodigal.

---

4 SRP- Original composition of Stephen Phifer

Let it be a place where relationships are formed and maintained as forgiveness flows to us as we let it flow to others, healing flows as a mighty river; revelation dawns and attitudes are changed.

Here, may the plow of worship break up the fallow ground of the hardest heart, may tears water the seed of the Word sown therein and may discipline, in the Father's strong and loving hands, steady us.

In this worship hall, let the talented serve and may only the servant shine. Let the music of the highest heaven shake the foundations of the lowest hell and Heaven's sweetest harmonies soothe the clamor of a fallen creation. May Sabbath rest blanket the weary soul.

Here, O Sovereign Lord, in this Your dwelling place, children laugh and God smiles; men kneel and God gives strength; women travail and God gives new life. In the Mighty Name of Jesus, the Sovereign Lord, we all agree. *Amen!*

Take your personal needs before the Lord through extemporaneous prayer.

Closing Prayer of Petition
BCP
Show us Your mercy, O Lord; And grant us Your salvation. Clothe Your ministers with righteousness: Let Your people sing with joy. Give peace, O Lord, in all the world; For only in You can we live in safety. Lord, keep this nation under Your care; And guide us in the way of justice and truth. Let Your way be known upon earth, Your saving health among all nations. Let not the needy, O Lord, be forgotten; Nor the hope of the poor be taken away. Create in us clean hearts, O God; And sustain us by Your Holy Spirit. *Amen.*

Confessions of Faith

The Apostles' Creed
BCP *(adaptation mine)*
I believe in God, the Father almighty, Creator of heaven and earth. I believe in Jesus Christ, His only Son, our Lord. He was conceived by the power of the Holy Spirit and born of the Virgin Mary. He suffered under Pontius Pilate, was crucified, died, and was buried. He descended

to the dead. On the third day he rose again. He ascended into heaven and is seated at the right hand of the Father. He will come again to judge the living and the dead. I believe in the Holy Spirit, the holy Christian Church, the communion of saints, the forgiveness of sins, the resurrection of the body, and the life everlasting. *Amen.*

Burden Casting Confession
From Psalm 55:22 and 1 Peter 5:6-7 (adapted from NKJV)

Today, I cast my burden upon You, Lord. You will sustain me. As I stand in the righteousness of Jesus, You will never permit me to be shaken, to slip, or to fall. Therefore, I humble myself under Your mighty hand, O God. Exalt me in due time. I cast all my care upon You, for You care for me.

Renewal Confession
Isaiah 40:28-31, **NIV**

Do you not know? Have you not heard? The LORD is the everlasting God, the Creator of the ends of the earth. He will not grow tired or weary, and his understanding no one can fathom.

He gives strength to the weary and increases the power of the weak. Even youths grow tired and weary, and young men stumble and fall; but those who hope in the LORD will renew their strength. They will soar on wings like eagles; they will run and not grow weary; they will walk and not be faint.

Psalm 52:8-9, **NIV**

But I am like an olive tree flourishing in the house of God; I trust in God's unfailing love for ever and ever. For what you have done I will praise you in the presence of your faithful people. And I will hope in your name, for your name is good.

Benediction

BCP

Lord Jesus Christ, You stretched out Your arms of love on the hard wood of the cross that everyone might come within the reach of Your saving embrace: So clothe us in Your Spirit that we, reaching forth our hands in love, may bring those who do not know You to the knowledge and love of You; for the honor of your Name. *Amen.*

Ephesians 3:20–21 (adapted from the KJV)
Now unto Him who is able to do exceeding abundantly above all that we ask or think, according to the power at work in us, Unto Him be glory in the church by Christ Jesus throughout all ages, world without end. *Amen.*

7 DAYS OF PRAYER

Monday

Invocation

(Before Worship)
BCP *(adaptation mine)*
O Almighty God, who pours out on all who desire it the spirit of grace and of supplication: Deliver me as I draw near to You, from coldness of heart and wanderings of mind, that with steadfast thoughts and kindled affections I may worship You in spirit and in truth; through Jesus Christ our Lord. *Amen.*

Psalm 43:3
BCP
Send out Your light and Your truth, that they may lead me, and bring me to Your holy hill and to Your dwelling.

Call to Worship

Titus 1:4, **NIV**
Grace and peace from God the Father and Christ Jesus our Savior.

BCP
The earth is the Lord's for He made it: Come let us adore Him.

In a short season of silence, draw away from the world and draw near to the Lord Jesus.

Confessions of Praise

The First Song of Isaiah
Isaiah 12:2–6
BCP

Surely, it is God who saves me; I will trust in Him and not be afraid. For the Lord is my stronghold and my sure defense, and He will be my Savior. Therefore, you *(I, we)* shall draw water with rejoicing from the springs of salvation. And on that day, you *(I, we)* shall say, Give thanks to the Lord and call upon His Name; Make His deeds known among the peoples; see that they remember that His Name is exalted. Sing praises of the Lord, for He has done great things, and this is known in all the world. Cry aloud, inhabitants of Zion, ring out your joy, for the great one in the midst of you is the Holy One of Israel.

Psalm 95:1–7, **NIV**

Come, let us sing for joy to the LORD; let us shout aloud to the Rock of our salvation. Let us come before him with thanksgiving and extol him with music and song. For the LORD is the great God, the great King above all gods. In His hand are the depths of the earth, and the mountain peaks belong to him. The sea is his, for he made it, and his hands formed the dry land. Come, let us bow down in worship, let us kneel before the LORD our Maker; for he is our God and we are the people of his pasture, the flock under his care.

Glory to the Father, and to the Son, and to the Holy Spirit: As it was in the beginning, is now, and will be forever. *Amen.*

Confessions of Worship

Colossians 1:15–20, (adapted from the NIV)
You, Lord Jesus, are the image of the invisible God, the firstborn over all creation. For by You all things were created: things in heaven and on earth, visible and invisible, whether thrones or powers or rulers or authorities; all things were created by You and for You. You are before all things, and in You all things hold together. And You are the head of the

body, the church; You are the beginning and the firstborn from among the dead, so that in everything You might have the supremacy. For the Father was pleased to have all His fullness dwell in You, and through You to reconcile to Himself all things, whether things on earth or things in heaven, by making peace through Your blood, shed on the cross.

Glory to the Father, and to the Son, and to the Holy Spirit: As it was in the beginning, is now, and will be forever. *Amen.*

A Song to the Lamb
Revelation 4:11, 5:9-10, 13
BCP
Splendor and honor and kingly power are Yours by right, O Lord our God, For You created everything that is, and by Your will they were created and have their being; and Yours by right, O Lamb that was slain, for with Your blood You have redeemed for God, From every family, language, people, and nation, a kingdom of priests to serve our God. And so, to Him who sits upon the throne, and to Christ the Lamb, be worship and praise, dominion and splendor, forever and for evermore.

Canticles of Worship

A Song of Creation
BCP
Invocation
Glorify the Lord, all you works of the Lord, praise Him and highly exalt Him forever. In the firmament of His power, glorify the Lord, praise him and highly exalt Him forever.

I. The Cosmic Order
Glorify the Lord, you angels and all powers of the Lord, O heavens and all waters above the heavens. Sun and moon and stars of the sky, glorify the Lord, praise him and highly exalt him forever. Glorify the Lord, every shower of rain and fall of dew, all winds and fire and heat. Winter and Summer, glorify the Lord, praise him and highly exalt him forever. Glorify the Lord, O chill and cold, drops of dew and flakes of snow. Frost and cold, ice and sleet, glorify the Lord, praise him and highly exalt him

forever. Glorify the Lord, O nights and days, O shining light and enfolding dark. Storm clouds and thunderbolts, glorify the Lord, praise Him and highly exalt Him forever.

Doxology
Let us glorify the Lord: Father, Son, and Holy Spirit. In the firmament of His power, glorify the Lord, Praise Him and highly exalt Him forever.

A Song of Praise
BCP
Glory to you, Lord God of our fathers; you are worthy of praise; glory to you. Glory to you for the radiance of your holy Name; we will praise you and highly exalt you forever.

Prayers of Repentance

BCP *(adaptation mine)*
Most merciful God, I confess that I have sinned against You in thought, word, and deed, by what I have done, and by what I have left undone. I have not loved You with my whole heart; I have not loved my neighbor as myself. I am truly sorry and I humbly repent. For the sake of Your Son Jesus Christ have mercy on me and forgive me; that I may delight in Your will, and walk in Your ways, to the glory of Your Name. *Amen.*

Almighty God has mercy on me. He forgives me all my sins through our Lord Jesus Christ. He strengthens me in all goodness, and by the power of the Holy Spirit keeps me in eternal life. *Amen.*

Scriptures for the Day

BCP *(adaptation mine)*
Lord, open my lips and my mouth shall proclaim Your praise.

Glory to the Father, and to the Son, and to the Holy Spirit: As it was in the beginning, is now, and will be forever. *Amen.*

The Psalms

Prayerfully read Psalms selected for the day or in sequence.

(At the end of the Psalms)
Glory to the Father, and to the Son, and to the Holy Spirit: As it was in the beginning, is now, and will be forever. *Amen.*

During a time of silence and listening prayer reflect on the passages you have read.

Old Testament Reading

Systemically read passages from Old Testament books.

(Before the Reading)
Hope in the Word
***Psalm 119:73-74*, NIV**
Your hands made me and formed me; give me understanding to learn your commands. May those who fear you rejoice when they see me, for I have put my hope in your Word.

(After the Reading)
The Word of the Lord. Thanks be to God.

During a time of silence and listening prayer reflect on the passages you have read.

New Testament Reading

Systemically read passages from New Testament Books.

(Before the Reading)
Prayer for Spiritual Vision
***Ephesians 1:17-19*, (adapted from the NIV)**
O glorious Father, give me the Spirit of wisdom and revelation, so that I may know You better. I pray also that the eyes of my heart may be enlightened in order that I may know the hope to which You have called me, the riches

of my glorious inheritance in the saints, and Your incomparably great power for us who believe.

(After the Reading)
The Word of the Lord. Thanks be to God.

During a time of silence and listening prayer, reflect on the passages you have read.

Prayers of Petition

The Lord's Prayer
BCP
Our Father in heaven, hallowed be Your Name, Your kingdom come, Your will be done, on earth as in heaven. Give us today our daily bread. Forgive us our sins as we forgive those who sin against us. Save us from the time of trial and deliver us from evil. For the kingdom, the power, and the glory are Yours, now and forever. *Amen.*

For Mondays
O Lord, Creator of time itself: sanctify this day for Your purposes. Give me clarity of thought and powers of concentration. I ask that You help this week to start well. Be with me in every conversation, every meeting, and make me a blessing to all; all this for the glory of Your name. *Amen.*

A Prayer for a Meaningful Life
Philippians 3:17–4:1 (adapted from the NLT)
You are my God, not my appetite. I praise You and boast of eternal and beautiful things. I am a citizen of heaven, where You, Lord Jesus live. And I am eagerly waiting for You to return as my Savior. Until then, You are taking my weak mortal body and changing it into a glorious body like your own, using the same mighty power that You will use to conquer everything, everywhere.

Prayers for Freedom and Discipline
1 Corinthians 9:24–27 (adapted from the NLT)
Lord, I remember that in a race everyone runs, but only one person gets the prize. I also must run in such a way that I will win. Athletes practice strict self-control. They do it to win a prize that will fade away, but we

do it for an eternal prize. So, I run straight to the goal with purpose in every step. I am not like a boxer who misses his punches. I discipline my body like an athlete, training it to do what it should. Otherwise, I fear that after preaching to others I myself might be disqualified.

Ephesians 5:29-3 (adapted from the NIV)
After all, no one ever hated his own body, but he feeds and cares for it, just as Christ does the church-for we are members of His body. I go from this place of prayer, full of the Holy Spirit and power, to live a disciplined life today, free from the bondage of the past, free from the chains of appetite, and healed from the wounds of my history.

Prayer for Courage
***2 Chronicles 15:7** (adapted from the ESV)*
(The Lord says,) "But you, take courage! Do not let your hands be weak. For your work shall be rewarded." I draw courage from You, Lord. My hands are strong, and my reward is on its way.

Take your personal needs before the Lord through extemporaneous prayer.

The General Thanksgiving
BCP
Almighty God, Father of all mercies, we Your unworthy servants give You humble thanks for all Your goodness and loving-kindness to us and to all whom You have made. We bless You for our creation, preservation, and all the blessings of this life; but above all for Your immeasurable love in the redemption of the world by our Lord Jesus Christ; for the means of grace, and for the hope of glory. And, we pray, give us such an awareness of Your mercies, that with truly thankful hearts we may show forth Your praise, not only with our lips, but in our lives, by giving up ourselves to Your service, and by walking before You in holiness and righteousness all our days; through Jesus Christ our Lord, to whom, with You and the Holy Spirit, be honor and glory throughout all ages. *Amen.*

Confessions of Faith

The Apostles' Creed
BCP *(adaptation mine)*
I believe in God, the Father almighty, Creator of heaven and earth. I believe in Jesus Christ, His only Son, our Lord. He was conceived by the power of the Holy Spirit and born of the Virgin Mary. He suffered under Pontius Pilate, was crucified, died, and was buried. He descended to the dead. On the third day He rose again. He ascended into heaven and is seated at the right hand of the Father. He will come again to judge the living and the dead. I believe in the Holy Spirit, the holy Christian Church, the communion of saints, the forgiveness of sins, the resurrection of the body, and the life everlasting. *Amen.*

Confession of Faith in the Father's Care
Mathew 6:25-33 *(adapted from the NLT)*
I do not worry about everyday life — whether I have enough food, drink, and clothes. Doesn't life consist of more than food and clothing? I look at the birds. They don't need to plant or harvest or put food in barns because You, my heavenly Father, feed them. And I am far more valuable to You than they are. Can all my worries add a single moment to my life? Of course not.

Fruitfulness Confession
Psalm 52:8-9, NIV
… I am like an olive tree flourishing in the house of God; I trust in God's unfailing love for ever and ever. For what you have done I will always praise you in the presence of your faithful people. And I will hope in your name, for your name is good. *Amen.*

Burden Casting Confession
Psalm 55:22 and 1 Peter 5:6-7 *(adapted from the NKJV)*
Today, I cast my burden upon You, Lord. You will sustain me. As I stand in the righteousness of Jesus, You will never permit me to be shaken, to slip, or to fall. Therefore, I humble myself under Your mighty hand, O God. Exalt me in due time. I cast all my care upon You, for You care for me.

Confession of Mercy and Blessing
Psalm 90:13–91:1 (adapted from the NLT)
Lord Jesus, You come to me in mercy; Your love is my portion today. As this day begins, I feast on Your truth and presence and I will joyfully sing throughout the day and night of Your unfailing love. Give us gladness in proportion to our former misery! Replace the evil years with good. Let us see Your miracles again; let our children see Your glory at work. And, Lord, show us Your approval and make our efforts successful. Yes, make our efforts successful!

I Am Not Ashamed
Romans 1:16–17; 1 Timothy 4:12–16; 2 Timothy 1:12 (adapted from the NKJV)
I am not ashamed of the gospel, because it is the power of God for the salvation of everyone who believes. For in the gospel a righteousness from God is revealed, one that is by faith from first to last, just as it is written: *"The righteous will live by faith."*

I will be an example to the believers in word, in conduct, in love, in spirit, in faith, in purity. I will give attention to reading, to exhortation, and to doctrine. I will not neglect God's gifts in me. I will meditate on these things; give myself entirely to them so that my progress may be evident to all. I will be careful that what I say and what I do agree, for in doing this, I will find my own salvation and be a blessing to those who hear me.

I am not ashamed, for I know whom I have believed and am persuaded that He is able to keep what I have committed to Him until that Day.

Benediction

BCP
Lord Jesus Christ, You stretched out Your arms of love on the hard wood of the cross that everyone might come within the reach of Your saving embrace: So clothe us in Your Spirit that we, reaching forth our hands in love, may bring those who do not know You to the knowledge and love of You; for the honor of your Name. *Amen.*

Ephesians 3:20–21 *(adaptation mine)*
Now unto Him who is able to do exceeding abundantly above all that we ask or think, according to the power at work in us, Unto Him be glory in the church by Christ Jesus throughout all ages, world without end. *Amen.*

7 DAYS OF PRAYER
Tuesday

Invocation

(Before Worship)
BCP *(adaptation mine)*
O Almighty God, who pours out on all who desire it the spirit of grace and of supplication: Deliver me as I draw near to You, from coldness of heart and wanderings of mind, that with steadfast thoughts and kindled affections I may worship You in spirit and in truth; through Jesus Christ our Lord. Amen

Psalm 43:3
BCP
Send out Your light and Your truth, that they may lead me, and bring me to Your holy hill and to Your dwelling.

Call to Worship

Psalm 122:1
BCP
I was glad when they said to me, *"Let us go to the house of the Lord."*

BCP
Worship the Lord in the beauty of holiness: Come let us adore Him.

In a short season of silence, draw away from the world and draw near to the Lord Jesus

Confessions of Praise

The Second Song of Isaiah
Isaiah 55:6–11
BCP

Seek the Lord while He wills to be found; Call upon Him when He draws near. Let the wicked forsake their ways and the evil ones their thoughts; And let them turn to the Lord, and He will have compassion, and to our God, for He will richly pardon. For My thoughts are not your thoughts, nor your ways My ways, says the Lord. For as the heavens are higher than the earth, so are My ways higher than your ways, and My thoughts than your thoughts. For as rain and snow fall from the heavens and return not again, but water the earth, bringing forth life and giving growth, seed for sowing and bread for eating, So is My Word that goes forth from My mouth; it will not return to Me empty; But it will accomplish that which I have purposed, and prosper in that for which I sent it.

Psalm 96, **NIV**

Sing to the LORD a new song; sing to the LORD, all the earth. Sing to the LORD, praise His name; proclaim His salvation day after day. Declare His glory among the nations, his marvelous deeds among all peoples. For great is the LORD and most worthy of praise; he is to be feared above all gods. For all the gods of the nations are idols, but the LORD made the heavens. Splendor and majesty are before Him; strength and glory are in his sanctuary.

Ascribe to the LORD, all you families of nations, ascribe to the LORD glory and strength. Ascribe to the LORD the glory due his name; bring an offering and come into his courts. Worship the LORD in the splendor of his holiness; tremble before him, all the earth. Say among the nations, "The LORD reigns. "The world is firmly established; it cannot be moved; he will judge the peoples with equity.

Let the heavens rejoice, let the earth be glad; let the sea resound, and all that is in it; let the fields be jubilant, and everything in them; let all the trees of the forest sing for joy; they will sing before the LORD, for He comes, he comes to judge the earth. He will judge the world in righteousness and the peoples in his faithfulness.

Glory to the Father, and to the Son, and to the Holy Spirit: As it was in the beginning, is now, and will be forever. *Amen.*

Confessions of Worship

The Highest Name
Ephesians 1:17–23 (adapted from the NKJV)
Father, I ask that You may give me the Spirit of wisdom and revelation, so that I may know Jesus better. I pray also that the eyes of my heart may be enlightened in order that I may know the hope to which You have called me, the riches of my glorious inheritance in the saints, and Your incomparably great power for us who believe. That power is like the working of Your mighty strength, which You exerted in Christ when You raised Him from the dead and seated Him at Your right hand in the heavenly realms, far above all rule and authority, power and dominion, and every title that can be given, not only in the present age but also in the one to come. Father, You placed all things under His feet and appointed Him to be head over everything for the church, which is His body, the fullness of Him who fills everything in every way.

Glory to the Father, and to the Son, and to the Holy Spirit: As it was in the beginning, is now, and will be forever. *Amen.*

The Song of the Redeemed
Revelation 15:3–4
BCP
O ruler of the universe, Lord God, great deeds are they that You have done, surpassing human understanding. Your ways are ways of righteousness and truth, O King of all the ages. Who can fail to do you homage, Lord, and sing the praises of Your Name? for You only are the Holy One. All nations will draw near and fall down before You, because Your just and holy works have been revealed.

Glory to the Father, and to the Son, and to the Holy Spirit: As it was in the beginning, is now, and will be forever. *Amen.*

Canticles of Worship

A Song of Creation
BCP
Invocation
Glorify the Lord, all you works of the Lord, praise Him and highly exalt Him forever. In the firmament of His power, glorify the Lord, praise Him and highly exalt Him forever.

II. The Earth and its Creatures
Let the earth glorify the Lord. Glorify the Lord, O mountains and hills, and all that grows upon the earth, praise Him and highly exalt Him forever. Glorify the Lord, O springs of water, seas, and streams, O whales and all that move in the waters. All birds of the air, glorify the Lord, praise Him and highly exalt Him forever. Glorify the Lord, O beasts of the wild, and all you flocks and herds. O men and women everywhere, glorify the Lord, praise Him and highly exalt Him forever.

Doxology
Let us glorify the Lord: Father, Son, and Holy Spirit. In the firmament of his power, glorify the Lord, Praise Him and highly exalt Him forever.

A Song of Praise
Glory to You in the splendor of Your temple; on the throne of Your majesty, glory to You. Glory to You, seated between the Cherubim; we will praise You and highly exalt You forever.

Prayers of Repentance

BCP *(adaptation mine)*
Most merciful God, I confess that I have sinned against You in thought, word, and deed, by what I have done, and by what I have left undone. I have not loved You with my whole heart; I have not loved my neighbor as myself. I am truly sorry and I humbly repent. For the sake of Your Son Jesus Christ have mercy on me and forgive me; that I may delight in Your will, and walk in Your ways, to the glory of Your Name. *Amen.*

Almighty God has mercy on me. He forgives me all my sins through our Lord Jesus Christ. He strengthens me in all goodness, and by the power of the Holy Spirit keeps me in eternal life. *Amen.*

Scriptures for the Day

BCP *(adaptation mine)*
Lord, open my lips and my mouth shall proclaim Your praise.

Glory to the Father, and to the Son, and to the Holy Spirit: As it was in the beginning, is now, and will be forever. *Amen.*

The Psalms

Prayerfully read Psalms selected for the day or in sequence.

(At the end of the Psalms)
Glory to the Father, and to the Son, and to the Holy Spirit: As it was in the beginning, is now, and will be forever. *Amen.*

During a time of silence and listening prayer, reflect on the passages you have read.

Old Testament Reading

Systemically read passages from Old Testament books.

(Before the Reading)
Hope in the Word
Psalm 119:73-74, **NIV**
Your hands made me and formed me; give me understanding to learn your commands. May those who fear you rejoice when they see me, for I have put my hope in your Word.

(After the Reading)
The Word of the Lord. Thanks be to God.

During a time of silence and listening prayer reflect on the passages you have read.

New Testament Reading

Systemically read passages from New Testament Books.

(Before the Reading)
Prayer for Spiritual Vision
Ephesians 1:17-19 *(adapted from the NIV)*
O glorious Father, give me the Spirit of wisdom and revelation, so that I may know You better. I pray also that the eyes of my heart may be enlightened in order that I may know the hope to which You have called me, the riches of my glorious inheritance in the saints, and Your incomparably great power for us who believe.

(After the Reading)
The Word of the Lord. Thanks be to God.

During a time of silence and listening prayer, reflect on the passages you have read.

Prayers of Petition

The Lord's Prayer
BCP
Our Father in heaven, hallowed be Your Name, Your kingdom come, Your will be done, on earth as in heaven. Give us today our daily bread. Forgive us our sins as we forgive those who sin against us. Save us from the time of trial and deliver us from evil. For the kingdom, the power, and the glory are Yours, now and forever. *Amen.*

For Tuesdays
Father in Heaven, Master of all time and space: bless my work today, making my life as fruitful as You have promised. Above this, bless my

relationships with those I contact today. Let me move at the impulse of Your love and in the integrity of Your heart. Help me honor You in everything I say and do, for Your everlasting glory. *Amen.*

Prayer of Stillness and Trust
Psalm 46:10; Ps 37:1-7 *(adapted from the NIV)*
"Be still and know that I am God; I will be exalted among the nations. I will be exalted in the earth." Don't worry about the wicked. Don't envy those who do wrong. For like grass, they soon fade away. Like springtime flowers, they soon wither.

I will trust in the LORD and do good. Then I will live safely in the land and prosper. I will take delight in the LORD, and He will give me my heart's desires.

I commit everything I do to the LORD. I trust him, and he will help me. He will make my innocence as clear as the dawn, and the justice of my cause will shine like the noonday sun.

Prayers for Freedom and Discipline
1 Corinthians 9:24-27 *(adapted from the NLT)*
Lord, I remember that in a race everyone runs, but only one person gets the prize. I also must run in such a way that I will win. Athletes practice strict self-control. They do it to win a prize that will fade away, but we do it for an eternal prize. So, I run straight to the goal with purpose in every step. I am not like a boxer who misses his punches. I discipline my body like an athlete, training it to do what it should. Otherwise, I fear that after preaching to others, I myself might be disqualified.

Romans 12:1-2 *(adapted from the NIV)*
Therefore, I offer my body as a living sacrifice, holy and pleasing to God-this is my spiritual act of worship. I do not conform any longer to the pattern of this world, but I am being transformed by the renewing of my mind. Then I will be able to test and approve what God's will is-His good, pleasing and perfect will.

I go from this place of prayer, full of the Holy Spirit and power, to live a disciplined life today, free from the bondage of the past, free from the chains of appetite, and healed from the wounds of my history.

Lord Jesus, You have broken the chains.
Philippians 2:13–18 *(adapted from the NKJV)*
Lord Jesus, You have broken the chains. You are at work in me both *"to will and to act according to Your good purpose."* I will not complain. I will not argue. I will be blameless and pure, a child of God without fault in a crooked and depraved generation. I shine like a star in the black sky. I hold out the Word of Life. I labor for Your reward. Though I am poured out like a drink-offering for the sacrifice and service of Your church, I will be glad and rejoice with Your church. Your church will be glad and rejoice with me. The substance, image, and reflection of my life shall be one in the same and this tree will sprout leaves today.

Take your personal needs before the Lord through extemporaneous prayer.

Closing Prayer
BCP
Show us Your mercy, O Lord; And grant us Your salvation. Clothe Your ministers with righteousness: Let Your people sing with joy. Give peace, O Lord, in all the world; For only in You can we live in safety. Lord, keep this nation under Your care; And guide us in the way of justice and truth. Let Your way be known upon earth, Your saving health among all nations. Let not the needy, O Lord, be forgotten; Nor the hope of the poor be taken away. Create in us clean hearts, O God; And sustain us by Your Holy Spirit. *Amen.*

Confessions of Faith

The Apostles' Creed
BCP *(adaptation mine)*
I believe in God, the Father almighty, Creator of heaven and earth. I believe in Jesus Christ, His only Son, our Lord. He was conceived by the power of the Holy Spirit and born of the Virgin Mary. He suffered under Pontius Pilate, was crucified, died, and was buried. He descended to the dead. On the third day He rose again. He ascended into heaven and is seated at the right hand of the Father. He will come again to judge the living and the dead. I believe in the Holy Spirit, the holy Christian Church,

the communion of saints, the forgiveness of sins, the resurrection of the body, and the life everlasting. *Amen.*

Confession of Faith in the Father's Care
Matthew 6:25–33 *(adapted from the NLT)*
I do not worry about my clothes. I look at the lilies and how they grow. They don't work or make their clothing, yet Solomon in all his glory was not dressed as beautifully as they are. And if You care so wonderfully for flowers that are here today and gone tomorrow, won't You more surely care for me? I have enough faith to receive Your constant care.

Fruitfulness Confession
Psalm 52:8–9, **NIV**
I am like an olive tree flourishing in the house of God; I trust in God's unfailing love for ever and ever. For what you have done I will always praise you in the presence of your faithful people. And I will hope in your name, for your name is good. *Amen.*

Burden Casting Confession
Psalm 55:22; 1 Peter 5:6–7 *(adapted from the NKJV)*
Today, I cast my burden upon You, Lord. You will sustain me. As I stand in the righteousness of Jesus, You will never permit me, to be shaken, to slip or to fall. Therefore, I humble myself under Your mighty hand, O God. Exalt me in due time. I cast all my care upon You, for You care for me.

Confession of Mercy and Blessing
Psalm 90:13–91:1 *(adapted from the NLT)*
Lord Jesus, You come to me in mercy; Your love is my portion today. As this day begins, I feast on Your truth and presence and I will joyfully sing throughout the day and night of Your unfailing love. Give us gladness in proportion to our former misery! Replace the evil years with good. Let us see Your miracles again; let our children see Your glory at work. And Lord, show us Your approval and make our efforts successful. Yes, make our efforts successful!

I Am Not Ashamed
Romans 1:16–17; 1 Timothy 4:12–16; 2 Timothy 1:12 (*adapted from the NKJV*)
I am not ashamed of the gospel, because it is the power of God for the salvation of everyone who believes. For in the gospel a righteousness from God is revealed, one that is by faith from first to last, just as it is written: *"The righteous will live by faith."*

I will be an example to the believers in word, in conduct, in love, in spirit, in faith, in purity. I will give attention to reading, to exhortation, and to doctrine. I will not neglect God's gifts in me. I will meditate on these things; give myself entirely to them so that my progress may be evident to all. I will be careful that what I say and what I do agree, for in doing this, I will find my own salvation and be a blessing to those who hear me.

I am not ashamed, for I know whom I have believed and am persuaded that He is able to keep what I have committed to Him until that Day.

Benediction

BCP
Lord Jesus Christ, You stretched out Your arms of love on the hard wood of the cross that everyone might come within the reach of Your saving embrace: So clothe us in Your Spirit that we, reaching forth our hands in love, may bring those who do not know You to the knowledge and love of You; for the honor of Your Name. *Amen.*

Ephesians 3:20–21 (*adapted from the KJV*)
Now unto Him who is able to do exceeding abundantly above all that we ask or think, according to the power at work in us, Unto Him be glory in the church by Christ Jesus throughout all ages, world without end. *Amen.*

7 DAYS OF PRAYER

Wednesday

Invocation

(Before Worship)
BCP *(adaptation mine)*
O Almighty God, who pours out on all who desire it the spirit of grace and of supplication: Deliver me as I draw near to You, from coldness of heart and wanderings of mind, that with steadfast thoughts and kindled affections I may worship You in spirit and in truth; through Jesus Christ our Lord. Amen

Psalm 43:3
BCP
Send out Your light and Your truth, that they may lead me, and bring me to Your holy hill and to Your dwelling.

Psalm 122:1
BCP
I was glad when they said to me, *"Let us go to the house of the Lord."*

Call to Worship

BCP
Worship the Lord in the beauty of holiness: Come let us adore Him.

In a short season of silence, draw away from the world and draw near to the Lord Jesus.

Confessions of Praise

The Third Song of Isaiah
Isaiah 60:1-3, 11a, 14c, 18-19
BCP

Arise, shine, for your light has come, and the glory of the Lord has dawned upon you. For behold, darkness covers the land; deep gloom enshrouds the peoples. But over you the Lord will rise, and His glory will appear upon you. Nations will stream to your light, and kings to the brightness of your dawning. Your gates will always be open; by day or night they will never be shut. They will call you, The City of the Lord, The Zion of the Holy One of Israel. Violence will no more be heard in your land, ruin or destruction within your borders. You will call your walls, Salvation, and all your portals, Praise. The sun will no more be your light by day; by night you will not need the brightness of the moon. The Lord will be your everlasting light, and your God will be your glory.

Psalm 97, **NIV**

The LORD reigns, let the earth be glad; let the distant shores rejoice. Clouds and thick darkness surround him; righteousness and justice are the foundation of his throne. Fire goes before him and consumes his foes on every side. His lightning lights up the world; the earth sees and trembles. The mountains melt like wax before the LORD, before the Lord of all the earth.

The heavens proclaim his righteousness, and all the peoples see his glory. All who worship images are put to shame, those who boast in idols—worship him, all you gods! Zion hears and rejoices, and the villages of Judah are glad because of your judgments, LORD. For you, LORD, are the Most High over all the earth; you are exalted far above all gods.

Let those who love the LORD hate evil, for he guards the lives of his faithful ones and delivers them from the hand of the wicked. Light shines upon the righteous and joy on the upright in heart. Rejoice in the LORD, you who are righteous, and praise his holy name.

Glory to the Father, and to the Son, and to the Holy Spirit: As it was in the beginning, is now, and will be forever. *Amen.*

Confessions of Worship

John's Testimony of Christ
John 1:1–5; 1 John 1:1–2; John 1:10–14, **NIV**

In the beginning was the Word, and the Word was with God, and the Word was God. He was with God in the beginning. Through him all things were made; without him nothing was made that has been made. In him was life, and that life was the light of mankind. The light shines in the darkness, but the darkness has not overcome it.

That which was from the beginning, which we have heard, which we have seen with our eyes, which we have looked at and our hands have touched—this we proclaim concerning the Word of life. The life appeared; we have seen it and testify to it, and we proclaim to you the eternal life, which was with the Father and has appeared to us.

He was in the world, and though the world was made through him, the world did not recognize him. He came to that which was his own, but his own did not receive him. Yet to all who received him, to those who believed in his name, he gave the right to become children of God—children born not of natural descent, nor of human decision or a husband's will, but born of God.

The Word became flesh and made His dwelling among us. We have seen His glory, the glory of the one and only Son, who came from the Father, full of grace and truth.

Glory to the Father, and to the Son, and to the Holy Spirit: As it was in the beginning, is now, and will be forever. *Amen.*

Glory to God
BCP

Glory to God in the highest, and peace to His people on earth. Lord God, heavenly King, almighty God and Father, we worship You, we give You thanks, we praise You for Your glory. Lord Jesus Christ, only Son of the Father, Lord God, Lamb of God, You take away the sin of the world: have mercy on us; You are seated at the right hand of the Father: receive our prayer. For You alone are the Holy One, You alone are the Lord, You alone are the Most High, Jesus Christ, with the Holy Spirit, in the glory of God the Father. *Amen.*

Glory to the Father, and to the Son, and to the Holy Spirit: As it was in the beginning, is now, and will be forever. *Amen.*

Canticles of Worship

A Song of Creation
BCP
Invocation
Glorify the Lord, all you works of the Lord, praise Him and highly exalt Him forever. In the firmament of His power, glorify the Lord, praise Him and highly exalt Him forever.

III. The People of God
Let the people of God glorify the Lord. Glorify the Lord, O priests and servants of the Lord, praise Him and highly exalt Him forever.

Glorify the Lord, O spirits and souls of the righteous. You that are holy and humble of heart, glorify the Lord, praise Him and highly exalt Him forever

Doxology
Let us glorify the Lord: Father, Son, and Holy Spirit. In the firmament of his power, glorify the Lord, Praise Him and highly exalt Him forever.

A Song of Praise
Glory to You in the splendor of Your temple; on the throne of Your majesty, glory to You. Glory to You, seated between the Cherubim; we will praise You and highly exalt You forever.

Prayers of Repentance

BCP *(adaptation mine)*
Most merciful God, I confess that I have sinned against You in thought, word, and deed, by what I have done, and by what I have left undone. I have not loved You with my whole heart; I have not loved my neighbor as myself. I am truly sorry and I humbly repent. For the sake of Your Son Jesus Christ have mercy on me and forgive me; that I may delight in Your will, and walk in Your ways, to the glory of Your Name. *Amen.*

Almighty God has mercy on me. He forgives me all my sins through our Lord Jesus Christ. He strengthens me in all goodness, and by the power of the Holy Spirit keeps me in eternal life. *Amen.*

Scriptures for the Day

BCP *(adaptation mine)*
Lord, open my lips and my mouth shall proclaim Your praise.

Glory to the Father, and to the Son, and to the Holy Spirit: As it was in the beginning, is now, and will be forever. *Amen.*

The Psalms

Prayerfully read Psalms selected for the day or in sequence.

(At the end of the Psalms)
Glory to the Father, and to the Son, and to the Holy Spirit: As it was in the beginning, is now, and will be forever. *Amen.*

During a time of silence and listening prayer, reflect on the passages you have read.

Old Testament Reading

Systemically read passages from Old Testament books.

(Before the Reading)
Hope in the Word
Psalm 119:73–74, NIV
Your hands made me and formed me; give me understanding to learn your commands. May those who fear you rejoice when they see me, for I have put my hope in your Word.

(After the Reading)
The Word of the Lord. Thanks be to God.

During a time of silence and listening prayer reflect on the passages you have read.

New Testament Reading

Systemically read passages from New Testament Books.

(Before the Reading)
Prayer for Spiritual Vision
Ephesians 1:17-19 *(adapted from the NIV)*
O glorious Father, give me the Spirit of wisdom and revelation, so that I may know You better. I pray also that the eyes of my heart may be enlightened in order that I may know the hope to which You have called me, the riches of my glorious inheritance in the saints, and Your incomparably great power for us who believe.

(After the Reading)
The Word of the Lord. Thanks be to God.

During a time of silence and listening prayer, reflect on the passages you have read.

Prayers of Petition

The Lord's Prayer
BCP
Our Father in heaven, hallowed be Your Name, Your kingdom come, Your will be done, on earth as in heaven. Give us today our daily bread. Forgive us our sins as we forgive those who sin against us. Save us from the time of trial and deliver us from evil. For the kingdom, the power, and the glory are Yours, now and forever. *Amen.*

For Wednesdays
Almighty God whose heartbeat is the rhythm of the universe: help me move in rhythm with You today. Lord, help all the things that have begun this week, to make progress today. You know the beginning from the ending of all things; You also know the middle of them. Bless relationships and

processes today so that this week may please You and all Your plans for us come to fruition. For You, Lord, all for You. *Amen.*

Prayer for Direction
Psalm 25:4–5, **NLT**
Show me the right path, O LORD; point out the road for me to follow. Lead me by your truth and teach me, for you are the God who saves me. All day long I put my hope in you.

Prayers for Freedom and Discipline
1 Corinthians 9:24–27 (adapted from the NLT)
Lord, I remember that in a race everyone runs, but only one person gets the prize. I also must run in such a way that I will win. Athletes practice strict self-control. They do it to win a prize that will fade away, but we do it for an eternal prize. So, I run straight to the goal with purpose in every step. I am not like a boxer who misses his punches. I discipline my body like an athlete, training it to do what it should. Otherwise, I fear that after preaching to others I myself might be disqualified.

Galatians 5:22 (adapted from the NLT)
The Holy Spirit controls my life. He is producing this kind of fruit in me: love, joy, peace, patience, kindness, goodness, faithfulness, gentleness, and self-control. Here there is no conflict with the law.

I go from this place of prayer, full of the Holy Spirit and power, to live a disciplined life today, free from the bondage of the past, free from the chains of appetite, and healed from the wounds of my history.

Lord Jesus, You have broken the chains.
Philippians 2:13–18 (adapted from the NKJV)
Lord Jesus, You have broken the chains. You are at work in me both to will and to act according to Your good purpose. I will not complain. I will not argue. I will be blameless and pure, a child of God without fault in a crooked and depraved generation. I shine like a star in the black sky. I hold out the Word of Life. I labor for Your reward. Though I am poured out like a drink-offering for the sacrifice and service of Your church, I will be glad and rejoice with Your church. Your church will be glad and

rejoice with me. The substance, image and reflection of my life shall be one in the same. And this tree will sprout leaves today.

Take your personal needs before the Lord through extemporaneous prayer.

The General Thanksgiving
BCP
Almighty God, Father of all mercies, we Your unworthy servants give You humble thanks for all Your goodness and loving-kindness to us and to all whom You have made. We bless You for our creation, preservation, and all the blessings of this life; but above all for Your immeasurable love in the redemption of the world by our Lord Jesus Christ; for the means of grace, and for the hope of glory. And, we pray, give us such an awareness of Your mercies, that with truly thankful hearts we may show forth Your praise, not only with our lips, but in our lives, by giving up ourselves to Your service, and by walking before you in holiness and righteousness all our days; through Jesus Christ our Lord, to whom, with You and the Holy Spirit, be honor and glory throughout all ages. *Amen.*

Confessions of Faith

The Apostles' Creed
BCP *(adaptation mine)*
I believe in God, the Father almighty, Creator of heaven and earth. I believe in Jesus Christ, His only Son, our Lord. He was conceived by the power of the Holy Spirit and born of the Virgin Mary. He suffered under Pontius Pilate, was crucified, died, and was buried. He descended to the dead. On the third day he rose again. He ascended into heaven and is seated at the right hand of the Father. He will come again to judge the living and the dead. I believe in the Holy Spirit, the holy Christian Church, the communion of saints, the forgiveness of sins, the resurrection of the body, and the life everlasting. *Amen.*

Confession of Faith in the Father's Care
Matt 6:25-33 (adapted from the NLT)
So I don't worry about having enough food or drink or clothing. Why be like the pagans who are so deeply concerned about these things? My

heavenly Father already knows all my needs, and You will give me all I need from day to day because I live for You and make the Kingdom of God my primary concern.

Fruitfulness Confession
Psalm 52:8-9, **NIV**
...I am like an olive tree flourishing in the house of God; I trust in God's unfailing love for ever and ever. For what you have done I will always praise you in the presence of your faithful people. And I will hope in your name, for your name is good. *Amen.*

Burden Casting Confession
Psalm 55:22; 1 Peter 5:6-7 (adapted from the NIV)
Today, I cast my burden upon You, Lord. You will sustain me. As I stand in the righteousness of Jesus, You will never permit me, to be shaken, to slip or to fall. Therefore, I humble myself under Your mighty hand, O God. Exalt me in due time. I cast all my care upon You, for You care for me.

Confession of Mercy and Blessing
Psalm 90:13-17 (adapted from the NLT)
Lord Jesus, You come to me in mercy; Your love is my portion today. As this day begins, I feast on Your truth and presence and I will joyfully sing throughout the day and night of Your unfailing love. Give us gladness in proportion to our former misery! Replace the evil years with good. Let us see Your miracles again; let our children see Your glory at work. And Lord, show us Your approval and make our efforts successful. Yes, make our efforts successful!

I Am Not Ashamed
Romans 1:16-17; 1 Timothy 4:12-16; 2 Timothy 1:12 (adapted from the NKJV)
I am not ashamed of the gospel, because it is the power of God for the salvation of everyone who believes. For in the gospel a righteousness from God is revealed, one that is by faith from first to last, just as it is written: *"The righteous will live by faith."*

I will be an example to the believers in word, in conduct, in love, in spirit, in faith, in purity. I will give attention to reading, to exhortation, and to doctrine. I will not neglect God's gifts in me. I will meditate on these things; give myself entirely to them so that my progress may be evident to all. I will be careful that what I say and what I do agree, for in doing this, I will find my own salvation and be a blessing to those who hear me.

I am not ashamed, for I know whom I have believed and am persuaded that He is able to keep what I have committed to Him until that Day.

Benediction

BCP
Lord Jesus Christ, You stretched out Your arms of love on the hard wood of the cross that everyone might come within the reach of Your saving embrace: So clothe us in Your Spirit that we, reaching forth our hands in love, may bring those who do not know You to the knowledge and love of You; for the honor of Your Name. *Amen.*

Ephesians 3:20–21 (adapted from the KJV)
Now unto Him who is able to do exceeding abundantly above all that we ask or think, according to the power at work in us, Unto Him be glory in the church by Christ Jesus throughout all ages, world without end. *Amen.*

7 DAYS OF PRAYER

Thursday

Invocation

(Before Worship)
BCP *(adaptation mine)*
O Almighty God, who pours out on all who desire it the spirit of grace and of supplication: Deliver me as I draw near to You, from coldness of heart and wanderings of mind, that with steadfast thoughts and kindled affections I may worship You in spirit and in truth; through Jesus Christ our Lord. *Amen.*

Psalm 43:3
BCP
Send out Your light and Your truth, that they may lead me, and bring me to Your holy hill and to Your dwelling.

Call of Worship

Psalm 122:1
BCP
I was glad when they said to me, *"Let us go to the house of the Lord."*

BCP
The earth is the Lord's for He made it: Come let us adore Him.

In a short season of silence, draw away from the world and draw near to the Lord Jesus.

Confessions of Praise

Isaiah 40:28-31, NIV
Do you not know? Have you not heard? The LORD is the everlasting God, the Creator of the ends of the earth. He will not grow tired or weary, and his understanding no one can fathom. He gives strength to the weary and increases the power of the weak. Even youths grow tired and weary, and young men stumble and fall; but those who hope in the LORD will renew their strength. They will soar on wings like eagles; they will run and not grow weary; they will walk and not be faint.

Psalm 98, NIV
Sing to the LORD a new song, for he has done marvelous things; his right hand and his holy arm have worked salvation for him. The LORD has made his salvation known and revealed his righteousness to the nations. He has remembered his love and his faithfulness to Israel; all the ends of the earth have seen the salvation of our God.

Shout for joy to the LORD, all the earth, burst into jubilant song with music; make music to the LORD with the harp, with the harp and the sound of singing, with trumpets and the blast of the ram's horn—shout for joy before the LORD, the King.

Let the sea resound, and everything in it, the world, and all who live in it. Let the rivers clap their hands, let the mountains sing together for joy; let them sing before the LORD, for he comes to judge the earth. He will judge the world in righteousness and the peoples with equity.

Glory to the Father, and to the Son, and to the Holy Spirit: As it was in the beginning, is now, and will be forever. *Amen.*

Confessions of Worship

You are God
BCP *(adaptation mine)*
You are God: we praise You; You are the Lord; we acclaim You; You are the eternal Father: All creation worships You. To You all angels, all the powers of heaven, Cherubim and Seraphim, sing in endless praise: Holy,

holy, holy Lord, God of power and might, heaven and earth are full of Your glory. The glorious company of apostles praises You. The noble fellowship of prophets praises You. The white-robed army of martyrs praises You. Throughout the world the holy Church acclaims you; Father, of majesty unbounded, Your true and only Son, worthy of all worship, and the Holy Spirit, advocate and guide.

You, Christ, are the King of glory, the eternal Son of the Father. When You became man to set us free You did not shun the Virgin's womb. You overcame the sting of death and opened the kingdom of heaven to all believers. You are seated at God's right hand in glory. We believe that you will come and be our judge. Come then, Lord, and help Your people, bought with the price of Your own blood, and bring us with Your saints to glory everlasting.

Glory to the Father, and to the Son, and to the Holy Spirit: As it was in the beginning, is now, and will be forever. *Amen.*

A Song to the Lamb
Revelation 4:11, 5:9-10, 13
BCP
Splendor and honor and kingly power are Yours by right, O Lord our God, For You created everything that is, and by Your will they were created and have their being; and Yours by right, O Lamb that was slain, for with Your blood You have redeemed for God, From every family, language, people, and nation, a kingdom of priests to serve our God. And so, to Him who sits upon the throne, and to Christ the Lamb, be worship and praise, dominion and splendor, forever and for evermore.

Glory to the Father, and to the Son, and to the Holy Spirit: As it was in the beginning, is now, and will be forever. *Amen.*

Canticles of Worship

A Song of Creation
BCP
Invocation
Glorify the Lord, all you works of the Lord, praise Him and highly exalt Him forever. In the firmament of his power, glorify the Lord, praise Him and highly exalt Him forever.

I. The Cosmic Order
Glorify the Lord, you angels and all powers of the Lord, O heavens and all waters above the heavens. Sun and moon and stars of the sky, glorify the Lord, praise Him and highly exalt Him forever Glorify the Lord, every shower of rain and fall of dew, all winds and fire and heat. Winter and Summer, glorify the Lord, praise Him and highly exalt Him forever. Glorify the Lord, O chill and cold, drops of dew and flakes of snow. Frost and cold, ice and sleet, glorify the Lord, praise Him and highly exalt Him forever. Glorify the Lord, O nights and days, O shining light and enfolding dark. Storm clouds and thunderbolts, glorify the Lord, praise Him and highly exalt Him forever.

Doxology
Let us glorify the Lord: Father, Son, and Holy Spirit. In the firmament of His power, glorify the Lord, praise Him and highly exalt Him forever.

A Song of Praise
Glory to You, Lord God of our fathers; You are worthy of praise; glory to You. Glory to You for the radiance of Your holy Name; we will praise You and highly exalt You forever.

Prayers of Repentance

BCP *(adaptation mine)*
Most merciful God, I confess that I have sinned against You in thought, word, and deed, by what I have done, and by what I have left undone. I have not loved You with my whole heart; I have not loved my neighbor as myself. I am truly sorry and I humbly repent. For the sake of Your Son

Jesus Christ have mercy on me and forgive me; that I may delight in Your will, and walk in Your ways, to the glory of your Name. *Amen.*

Almighty God has mercy on me. He forgives me all my sins through our Lord Jesus Christ. He strengthens me in all goodness, and by the power of the Holy Spirit keeps me in eternal life. *Amen.*

Scriptures for the Day

BCP *(adaptation mine)*
Lord, open my lips and my mouth shall proclaim Your praise.

Glory to the Father, and to the Son, and to the Holy Spirit: As it was in the beginning, is now, and will be forever. *Amen.*

The Psalms

Prayerfully read Psalms selected for the day or in sequence.

(At the end of the Psalms)
Glory to the Father, and to the Son, and to the Holy Spirit: As it was in the beginning, is now, and will be forever. *Amen.*

During a time of silence and listening prayer reflect on the passages you have read.

Old Testament Reading

Systemically read passages from Old Testament books.

(Before the Reading)
Hope in the Word
Psalm 119:73-74, **NIV**
Your hands made me and formed me; give me understanding to learn your commands. May those who fear you rejoice when they see me, for I have put my hope in your word.

(After the Reading)
The Word of the Lord. Thanks be to God.

During a time of silence and listening prayer reflect on the passages you have read.

New Testament Reading

Systemically read passages from New Testament Books.

(Before the Reading)
Prayer for Spiritual Vision
Ephesians 1:17-19 *(adapted from the NIV)*
O glorious Father, give me the Spirit of wisdom and revelation, so that I may know You better. I pray also that the eyes of my heart may be enlightened in order that I may know the hope to which You have called me, the riches of my glorious inheritance in the saints, and Your incomparably great power for us who believe.

(After the Reading)
The Word of the Lord. Thanks be to God.

During a time of silence and listening prayer reflect on the passages you have read.

Prayers of Petition

The Lord's Prayer
BCP
Our Father in heaven, hallowed be Your Name, your kingdom come, Your will be done, on earth as in heaven. Give us today our daily bread. Forgive us our sins as we forgive those who sin against us. Save us from the time of trial and deliver us from evil. For the kingdom, the power, and the glory are Yours, now and forever. *Amen.*

For Thursdays
Heavenly King, You are the joy of all the earth and the praise of heaven: I praise You for this week and all the things You are doing in my life and work

and for all the people You have placed in my life. Help me accept events and people today who seem to interrupt my work. Thank You for time at Your feet, like Mary of Bethany. Help me in life's kitchen, like Martha of Bethany; let my thoughts, words and deeds be pleasing to You. *Amen.*

Burden Casting Prayer
Psalm 55:22; 1 Peter 5:6-7 *(adapted from the NKJV)*
Today, I cast my burden upon You, Lord. You will sustain me. As I stand in the righteousness of Jesus, You will never permit me, to be shaken, to slip or to fall. Therefore, I humble myself under Your mighty hand, O God. Exalt me in due time. I cast all my care upon You, for You care for me. *Amen.*

Prayers for Freedom and Discipline
1 Corinthians 9:24-27 *(adapted from the NLT)*
Lord, I remember that in a race everyone runs, but only one person gets the prize. I also must run in such a way that I will win. Athletes practice strict self-control. They do it to win a prize that will fade away, but we do it for an eternal prize. So, I run straight to the goal with purpose in every step. I am not like a boxer who misses his punches. I discipline my body like an athlete, training it to do what it should. Otherwise, I fear that after preaching to others I myself might be disqualified.

1 Corinthians 15:57-58 *(adapted from the NIV)*
Thanks be to God! He gives us the victory through our Lord Jesus Christ. Therefore, I stand firm. I let nothing move me. I always give myself fully to the work of the Lord, I go from this place of prayer, full of the Holy Spirit and power, to live a disciplined life today, free from the bondage of the past, free from the chains of appetite, and healed from the wounds of my history.

Lord Jesus, You have broken the chains.
Philippians 2:13-18 *(adapted from the NKJV)*
Lord Jesus, You have broken the chains. You are at work in me both to will and to act according to Your good purpose. I will not complain. I will not argue. I will be blameless and pure, a child of God without fault in a crooked and depraved generation. I shine like a star in the black sky. I hold out the Word of Life. I labor for Your reward. Though I am poured

out like a drink-offering for the sacrifice and service of Your church, I will be glad and rejoice with Your church. Your church will be glad and rejoice with me. The substance, image and reflection of my life shall be one in the same. And this tree will sprout leaves today.

Take your personal needs before the Lord through extemporaneous prayer.

Closing Prayer
BCP
Show us Your mercy, O Lord; And grant us Your salvation. Clothe Your ministers with righteousness: Let Your people sing with joy. Give peace, O Lord, in all the world; For only in You can we live in safety. Lord, keep this nation under Your care; And guide us in the way of justice and truth. Let Your way be known upon earth, Your saving health among all nations. Let not the needy, O Lord, be forgotten; Nor the hope of the poor be taken away. Create in us clean hearts, O God; And sustain us by Your Holy Spirit. *Amen.*

Confessions of Faith

The Apostles' Creed
BCP *(adaptation mine)*
I believe in God, the Father almighty, Creator of heaven and earth. I believe in Jesus Christ, His only Son, our Lord. He was conceived by the power of the Holy Spirit and born of the Virgin Mary. He suffered under Pontius Pilate, was crucified, died, and was buried. He descended to the dead. On the third day he rose again. He ascended into heaven and is seated at the right hand of the Father. He will come again to judge the living and the dead. I believe in the Holy Spirit, the holy Christian Church, the communion of saints, the forgiveness of sins, the resurrection of the body, and the life everlasting. *Amen.*

Confession of Faith in the Father's Care
Matthew 6:25-33 *(adapted from the NLT)*
I do not worry about everyday life — whether I have enough food, drink, and clothes. Doesn't life consist of more than food and clothing? I look at the birds. They don't need to plant or harvest or put food in barns

because You, my heavenly Father, feed them. And I am far more valuable to You than they are. Can all my worries add a single moment to my life? Of course not.

Fruitfulness Confession
Psalm 52:8–9, **NIV**
…I am like an olive tree flourishing in the house of God; I trust in God's unfailing love for ever and ever. For what you have done I will always praise you in the presence of your faithful people. And I will hope in your name, for your name is good. *Amen.*

Burden Casting Confession
Psalm 55:22; 1 Peter 5:6–7 (adapted from the NKJV)
Today, I cast my burden upon You, Lord. You will sustain me. As I stand in the righteousness of Jesus, You will never permit me, to be shaken, to slip or to fall. Therefore, I humble myself under Your mighty hand, O God. Exalt me in due time. I cast all my care upon You, for You care for me.

Confession of Mercy and Blessing
Psalm 90:13–17 (adapted from the NLT)
Lord Jesus, You come to me in mercy; Your love is my portion today. As this day begins, I feast on Your truth and presence and I will joyfully sing throughout the day and night of Your unfailing love. Give us gladness in proportion to our former misery! Replace the evil years with good. Let us see Your miracles again; let our children see Your glory at work. And Lord, show us Your approval and make our efforts successful. Yes, make our efforts successful!

I Am Not Ashamed
Romans 1:16–17; 1 Timothy 4:12–16; 2 Timothy 1:12 (adapted from the NIV)
I am not ashamed of the gospel, because it is the power of God for the salvation of everyone who believes. For in the gospel a righteousness from God is revealed, one that is by faith from first to last, just as it is written: *"The righteous will live by faith."*

I will be an example to the believers in word, in conduct, in love, in spirit, in faith, in purity. I will give attention to reading, to exhortation, and to doctrine. I will not neglect God's gifts in me. I will meditate on these things; give myself entirely to them so that my progress may be evident to all. I will be careful that what I say and what I do agree, for in doing this, I will find my own salvation and be a blessing to those who hear me.

I am not ashamed, for I know whom I have believed and am persuaded that He is able to keep what I have committed to Him until that Day.

Benediction

BCP
Lord Jesus Christ, You stretched out Your arms of love on the hard wood of the cross that everyone might come within the reach of Your saving embrace: So clothe us in Your Spirit that we, reaching forth our hands in love, may bring those who do not know You to the knowledge and love of You; for the honor of Your Name. *Amen.*

Ephesians 3:20–21 (adapted from the KJV)
Now unto Him who is able to do exceeding abundantly above all that we ask or think, according to the power at work in us, Unto Him be glory in the church by Christ Jesus throughout all ages, world without end. *Amen.*

7 DAYS OF PRAYER

Friday

Invocation

(Before Worship)
BCP *(adaptation mine)*
O Almighty God, who pours out on all who desire it the spirit of grace and of supplication: Deliver me as I draw near to You, from coldness of heart and wanderings of mind, that with steadfast thoughts and kindled affections I may worship You in spirit and in truth; through Jesus Christ our Lord. *Amen.*

Psalm 43:3
BCP
Send out Your light and Your truth, that they may lead me, and bring me to Your holy hill and to Your dwelling.

Call to Worship

Psalm 122:1
BCP
I was glad when they said to me, *"Let us go to the house of the Lord."*

BCP
Worship the Lord in the beauty of holiness: Come let us adore Him.

In a short season of silence, draw away from the world and draw near to the Lord Jesus.

Confessions of Praise

Isaiah's Song of the Cross
***Isaiah 53:1–6*, NIV**

Who has believed our message and to whom has the arm of the LORD been revealed? He grew up before him like a tender shoot, and like a root out of dry ground. He had no beauty or majesty to attract us to him, nothing in his appearance that we should desire him. He was despised and rejected by mankind, a man of suffering, and familiar with pain. Like one from whom people hide their faces he was despised, and we held him in low esteem.

Surely, he took up our pain and bore our suffering, yet we considered him punished by God, stricken by him, and afflicted. But he was pierced for our transgressions, he was crushed for our iniquities; the punishment that brought us peace was on him, and by his wounds we are healed. We all, like sheep, have gone astray, each of us has turned to our own way; and the LORD has laid on him the iniquity of us all.

***Psalm 99*, NIV**

The LORD reigns, let the nations tremble; he sits enthroned between the cherubim, let the earth shake. Great is the LORD in Zion; he is exalted over all the nations. Let them praise your great and awesome name—he is holy.

The King is mighty, he loves justice—you have established equity: in Jacob you have done what is just and right. Exalt the LORD our God and worship at his footstool; he is holy.

Moses and Aaron were among his priests, Samuel was among those who called on his name; they called on the LORD and he answered them. He spoke to them from the pillar of cloud; they kept his statutes and the decrees he gave them.

LORD our God, you answered them; you were to Israel a forgiving God, though you punished their misdeeds. Exalt the LORD our God and worship at his holy mountain, for the LORD our God is holy.

Glory to the Father, and to the Son, and to the Holy Spirit: As it was in the beginning, is now, and will be forever. *Amen.*

Confessions of Worship

Psalm 24, **NIV**
The earth is the LORD's, and everything in it, the world, and all who live in it; for he founded it on the seas and established it on the waters.

Who may ascend the mountain of the LORD? Who may stand in his holy place? The one who has clean hands and a pure heart, who does not trust in an idol or swear by a false god.

They will receive blessing from the LORD and vindication from God their Savior. Such is the generation of those who seek him, who seek your face, God of Jacob.

Lift up your heads, you gates; be lifted up, you ancient doors, that the King of glory may come in. Who is this King of glory? The LORD strong and mighty, the LORD mighty in battle. Lift up your heads, you gates; lift them up, you ancient doors, that the King of glory may come in. Who is he, this King of glory? The LORD Almighty—he is the King of glory.

Glory to the Father, and to the Son, and to the Holy Spirit: As it was in the beginning, is now, and will be forever. *Amen.*

Colossians 1:15–20 (adapted from the NIV)
Lord Jesus, You are the image of the invisible God, the firstborn over all creation. For by You all things were created: things in heaven and on earth, visible and invisible, whether thrones or powers or rulers or authorities; all things were created by You and for You. You are before all things, and in You all things hold together. And You are the head of the body, the church; You are the beginning and the firstborn from among the dead, so that in everything You might have the supremacy. For God, the Father was pleased to have all his fullness dwell in You, and through You to reconcile to himself all things, whether things on earth or things in heaven, by making peace through Your blood, shed on the cross.

Canticles of Worship

A Song of Creation
BCP
Invocation
Glorify the Lord, all You works of the Lord, praise Him and highly exalt Him forever. In the firmament of His power, glorify the Lord, praise Him and highly exalt Him forever.

II. The Earth and its Creatures
Let the earth glorify the Lord. Glorify the Lord, O mountains and hills, and all that grows upon the earth, praise Him and highly exalt Him forever. Glorify the Lord, O springs of water, seas, and streams, O whales and all that move in the waters. All birds of the air, glorify the Lord, praise Him and highly exalt Him forever. Glorify the Lord, O beasts of the wild, and all you flocks and herds. O men and women everywhere, glorify the Lord, praise Him and highly exalt Him forever.

Doxology
Let us glorify the Lord: Father, Son, and Holy Spirit. In the firmament of his power, glorify the Lord, praise Him and highly exalt Him forever.

A Song of Praise
Glory to You, Lord God of our fathers; You are worthy of praise; glory to You. Glory to You for the radiance of Your holy Name; we will praise You and highly exalt You forever.

Prayers of Repentance

BCP *(adaptation mine)*
Most merciful God, I confess that I have sinned against You in thought, word, and deed, by what I have done, and by what I have left undone. I have not loved You with my whole heart; I have not loved my neighbor as myself. I am truly sorry and I humbly repent. For the sake of Your Son Jesus Christ have mercy on me and forgive me; that I may delight in Your will, and walk in Your ways, to the glory of Your Name. *Amen.*

Almighty God has mercy on me. He forgives me all my sins through our Lord Jesus Christ. He strengthens me in all goodness, and by the power of the Holy Spirit keeps me in eternal life. *Amen.*

Scriptures for the Day
BCP *(adaptation mine)*
Lord, open my lips and my mouth shall proclaim Your praise.

Glory to the Father, and to the Son, and to the Holy Spirit: As it was in the beginning, is now, and will be forever. *Amen.*

The Psalms Prayerfully read Psalms selected for the day or in sequence.

(At the end of the Psalms)
Glory to the Father, and to the Son, and to the Holy Spirit: As it was in the beginning, is now, and will be forever. *Amen.*

During a time of silence and listening prayer reflect on the passages you have read.

Old Testament Reading

Systemically read passages from Old Testament books.

(Before the Reading)
Hope in the Word
Psalm 119:73–74, NIV
Your hands made me and formed me; give me understanding to learn your commands. May those who fear you rejoice when they see me, for I have put my hope in your word.

(After the Reading)
The Word of the Lord. Thanks be to God.

During a time of silence and listening prayer reflect on the passages you have read.

New Testament Reading

Systemically read passages from New Testament Books.

(Before the Reading)
Prayer for Spiritual Vision
Ephesians 1:17–19 *(adapted from the NIV)*
O glorious Father, give me the Spirit of wisdom and revelation, so that I may know You better. I pray also that the eyes of my heart may be enlightened in order that I may know the hope to which You have called me, the riches of my glorious inheritance in the saints, and Your incomparably great power for us who believe.

(After the Reading)
The Word of the Lord. Thanks be to God.

During a time of silence and listening prayer reflect on the passages you have read.

Prayers of Petition

The Lord's Prayer
BCP
Our Father in heaven, hallowed be Your Name, your kingdom come, Your will be done, on earth as in heaven. Give us today our daily bread. Forgive us our sins as we forgive those who sin against us. Save us from the time of trial and deliver us from evil. For the kingdom, the power, and the glory are Yours, now and forever. *Amen.*

For Fridays
BCP
Almighty God, whose most dear Son went not up to joy but first He suffered pain, and entered not into glory before He was crucified: Mercifully grant that we, walking in the way of the cross, may find it none other than the way of life and peace; through Jesus Christ Your Son our Lord. *Amen.*

For Guidance
BCP
Heavenly Father, in You we live and move and have our being: We humbly pray You so to guide and govern us by Your Holy Spirit, that in all the cares and occupations of our life we may not forget You, but may remember that we are ever walking in Your sight; through Jesus Christ our Lord. *Amen.*

Prayers for Freedom and Discipline
1 Corinthians 9:24–27 (adapted from the NLT)
Lord, I remember that in a race everyone runs, but only one person gets the prize. I also must run in such a way that I will win. Athletes practice strict self-control. They do it to win a prize that will fade away, but we do it for an eternal prize. So, I run straight to the goal with purpose in every step. I am not like a boxer who misses his punches. I discipline my body like an athlete, training it to do what it should. Otherwise, I fear that after preaching to others I myself might be disqualified.

Romans 8:37–39 (adapted from the NKJV)
Yet in all these things we are more than conquerors through Him who loved us. For I am persuaded that neither death nor life, nor angels nor principalities nor powers, nor things present nor things to come, nor height nor depth, nor any other created thing, shall be able to separate us from the love of God which is in Christ Jesus our Lord.

Romans 12:1–2 (adapted from the NIV)
Therefore, I offer my body as a living sacrifice, holy and pleasing to God-this is my spiritual act of worship. I do not conform any longer to the pattern of this world, but I am being transformed by the renewing of my mind. Then I will be able to test and approve what God's will is-His good, pleasing and perfect will.

I go from this place of prayer, full of the Holy Spirit and power, to live a disciplined life today, free from the bondage of the past, free from the chains of appetite, and healed from the wounds of my history.

Lord Jesus, You have broken the chains.
Philippians 2:13–18 *(adapted from the NKJV)*
Lord Jesus, You have broken the chains. You are at work in me both to will and to act according to Your good purpose. I will not complain. I will not argue. I will be blameless and pure, a child of God without fault in a crooked and depraved generation. I shine like a star in the black sky. I hold out the Word of Life. I labor for Your reward. Though I am poured out like a drink-offering for the sacrifice and service of Your church, I will be glad and rejoice with Your church. Your church will be glad and rejoice with me. The substance, image, and reflection of my life shall be one in the same. And this tree will sprout leaves today.

Take your personal needs before the Lord through extemporaneous prayer.

The General Thanksgiving
BCP
Almighty God, Father of all mercies, we Your unworthy servants give You humble thanks for all Your goodness and loving-kindness to us and to all whom You have made. We bless You for our creation, preservation, and all the blessings of this life; but above all for Your immeasurable love in the redemption of the world by our Lord Jesus Christ; for the means of grace, and for the hope of glory. And, we pray, give us such an awareness of Your mercies, that with truly thankful hearts we may show forth Your praise, not only with our lips, but in our lives, by giving up ourselves to Your service, and by walking before You in holiness and righteousness all our days; through Jesus Christ our Lord, to whom, with You and the Holy Spirit, be honor and glory throughout all ages. Amen.

Confessions of Faith

The Apostles' Creed
BCP *(adaptation mine)*
I believe in God, the Father almighty, Creator of heaven and earth. I believe in Jesus Christ, His only Son, our Lord. He was conceived by the power of the Holy Spirit and born of the Virgin Mary. He suffered under Pontius Pilate, was crucified, died, and was buried. He descended to the dead. On the third day he rose again. He ascended into heaven and

is seated at the right hand of the Father. He will come again to judge the living and the dead. I believe in the Holy Spirit, the holy Christian Church, the communion of saints, the forgiveness of sins, the resurrection of the body, and the life everlasting. *Amen.*

Confession of Faith in the Father's Care
Matthew 6:25-33 (adapted from the NLT)
I do not worry about my clothes. I look at the lilies and how they grow. They don't work or make their clothing, yet Solomon in all his glory was not dressed as beautifully as they are. And if You care so wonderfully for flowers that are here today and gone tomorrow, won't You more surely care for me? I have enough faith to receive Your constant care.

Fruitfulness Confession
Psalm 52:8-9, **NIV**
…I am like an olive tree flourishing in the house of God; I trust in God's unfailing love for ever and ever. For what you have done I will always praise you in the presence of your faithful people. And I will hope in your name, for your name is good. *Amen.*

Burden Casting Confession
Psalm 55:22; 1 Peter 5:6-7 (adapted from the NKJV)
Today, I cast my burden upon You, Lord. You will sustain me. As I stand in the righteousness of Jesus, You will never permit me, to be shaken, to slip or to fall. Therefore, I humble myself under Your mighty hand, O God. Exalt me in due time. I cast all my care upon You, for You care for me.

Confession of Mercy and Blessing
Psalm 90:13-17 (adapted from the NLT)
Lord Jesus, You come to me in mercy; Your love is my portion today. As this day begins, I feast on Your truth and presence and I will joyfully sing throughout the day and night of Your unfailing love. Give us gladness in proportion to our former misery! Replace the evil years with good. Let us see Your miracles again; let our children see Your glory at work. And Lord, show us Your approval and make our efforts successful. Yes, make our efforts successful!

I Am Not Ashamed
Romans 1:16–17; 1 Timothy 4:12–16; 2 Timothy 1:12 *(adapted from the KJV)*
I am not ashamed of the gospel, because it is the power of God for the salvation of everyone who believes. For in the gospel a righteousness from God is revealed, one that is by faith from first to last, just as it is written: *"The righteous will live by faith."* I will be an example to the believers in word, in conduct, in love, in spirit, in faith, in purity. I will give attention to reading, to exhortation, and to doctrine. I will not neglect God's gifts in me. I will meditate on these things; give myself entirely to them so that my progress may be evident to all. I will be careful that what I say and what I do agree, for in doing this, I will find my own salvation and be a blessing to those who hear me. I am not ashamed, for I know whom I have believed and am persuaded that He is able to keep what I have committed to Him until that Day.

Benediction

BCP
Lord Jesus Christ, You stretched out Your arms of love on the hard wood of the cross that everyone might come within the reach of Your saving embrace: So clothe us in Your Spirit that we, reaching forth our hands in love, may bring those who do not know You to the knowledge and love of You; for the honor of Your Name. *Amen.*

Ephesians 3:20–21 (*adapted from the NIV*)
Now unto Him who is able to do exceeding abundantly above all that we ask or think, according to the power at work in us, Unto Him be glory in the church by Christ Jesus throughout all ages, world without end. *Amen.*

7 DAYS OF PRAYER
Saturday

Invocation / Call to Worship

Rejoice in the Lord!
Psalms 32:11; 64:10; 97:12; 104:34, **NIV**
Rejoice in the LORD and be glad, you righteous; sing, all you who are upright in heart!

The righteous will rejoice in the LORD and take refuge in him; all the upright in heart will glory in him!

Rejoice in the LORD, you who are righteous, and praise his holy name.

May my meditation be pleasing to him, as I rejoice in the LORD.

Joel 2:23–24, **NIV**
Be glad, people of Zion, rejoice in the LORD your God, for he has given you the autumn rains because he is faithful. He sends you abundant showers, both autumn and spring rains, as before. The threshing floors will be filled with grain; the vats will overflow with new wine and oil.

Philippians 4:4–7, **NIV**
Rejoice in the Lord always. I will say it again: Rejoice! Let your gentleness be evident to all. The Lord is near. Do not be anxious about anything, but in every situation, by prayer and petition, with thanksgiving, present your requests to God. And the peace of God, which transcends all understanding, will guard your hearts and your minds in Christ Jesus.

Psalm 33:20-22, **NIV**
We wait in hope for the LORD; he is our help and our shield. In him our hearts rejoice, for we trust in his holy name. May your unfailing love be with us, LORD, even as we put our hope in you.

Matthew 11:28-30, **NKJV**
"Come to me, all you who labor and are heavy laden, and I will give you rest. Take My yoke upon you and learn from Me, for I am gentle and lowly in heart, and you will find rest for your souls. For My yoke is easy and My burden is light."

In a short season of silence, draw away from the world and draw near to the Lord Jesus.

Confessions of Praise

Psalm 91:1-2, **NIV**
Whoever dwells in the shelter of the Most High will rest in the shadow of the Almighty. I will say of the LORD, *"He is my refuge and my fortress, my God, in whom I trust."*

Isaiah's Song of Peace
Isaiah 9:6-7; 26:1-4; 55:12-13; 60:16-17, **NIV**
For to us a child is born, to us a son is given, and the government will be on his shoulders. And he will be called Wonderful Counselor, Mighty God, Everlasting Father, Prince of Peace. Of the greatness of his government and peace there will be no end. He will reign on David's throne and over his kingdom, establishing and upholding it with justice and righteousness from that time on and forever. The zeal of the LORD Almighty will accomplish this.

In that day this song will be sung in the land of Judah: We have a strong city; God makes salvation its walls and ramparts. Open the gates that the righteous nation may enter, the nation that keeps faith. You will keep in perfect peace him whose minds are steadfast, because they trust in You. Trust in the LORD forever, for the LORD, the LORD himself, is the Rock eternal.

"You will go out in joy and be led forth in peace; the mountains and hills will burst into song before you, and all the trees of the field will clap their hands.

Instead of the thornbush will grow the juniper, and instead of briers the myrtle will grow. This will be for the LORD's renown, for an everlasting sign, that will endure forever."

Then you will know that I, the LORD, am your Savior, your Redeemer, the Mighty One of Jacob. Instead of bronze I will bring you gold, and silver in place of iron. Instead of wood I will bring you bronze, and iron in place of stones. I will make peace your governor and well-being your ruler.

***Psalm 149*, NIV**
Praise the LORD. Sing to the LORD a new song, his praise in the assembly of his faithful people. Let Israel rejoice in their Maker; let the people of Zion be glad in their King. Let them praise his name with dancing and make music to him with timbrel and harp. For the LORD takes delight in his people; he crowns the humble with victory. Let his faithful people rejoice in this honor and sing for joy on their beds. May the praise of God be in their mouths and a double-edged sword in their hands, to inflict vengeance on the nations and punishment on the peoples, to bind their kings with fetters, their nobles with shackles of iron, to carry out the sentence written against them—this is the glory of all his faithful people. Praise the LORD.

Glory to the Father, and to the Son, and to the Holy Spirit: As it was in the beginning, is now, and will be forever. *Amen.*

Confessions of Worship

***Psalm 24*, NIV**
The earth is the LORD's, and everything in it, the world, and all who live in it; for he founded it on the seas and established it on the waters.

Who may ascend the mountain of the LORD? Who may stand in his holy place? The one who has clean hands and a pure heart, who does not trust in an idol or swear by a false god.

They will receive blessing from the LORD and vindication from God their Savior. Such is the generation of those who seek him, who seek your face, God of Jacob.

Lift up your heads, you gates; be lifted up, you ancient doors, that the King of glory may come in. Who is this King of glory? The LORD strong and mighty, the LORD mighty in battle. Lift up your heads, you gates; lift them up, you ancient doors, that the King of glory may come in. Who is he, this King of glory? The LORD Almighty—he is the King of glory.

Glory to the Father, and to the Son, and to the Holy Spirit: As it was in the beginning, is now, and will be forever. *Amen.*

Colossians 1:15-20 (adapted from the NKJV)
Lord Jesus, You are the image of the invisible God, the firstborn over all creation. For by You all things were created: things in heaven and on earth, visible and invisible, whether thrones or powers or rulers or authorities; all things were created by You and for You. You are before all things, and in You all things hold together. And You are the head of the body, the church; You are the beginning and the firstborn from among the dead, so that in everything You might have the supremacy. For God, the Father was pleased to have all his fullness dwell in You, and through You to reconcile to himself all things, whether things on earth or things in heaven, by making peace through Your blood, shed on the cross.

Canticles of Worship

A Song of Creation
BCP
Invocation
Glorify the Lord, all you works of the Lord, praise Him and highly exalt Him forever. In the firmament of his power, glorify the Lord, praise Him and highly exalt Him forever.

II The Earth and its Creatures
Let the earth glorify the Lord. Glorify the Lord, O mountains and hills, and all that grows upon the earth, praise Him and highly exalt Him forever. Glorify the Lord, O springs of water, seas, and streams, O whales and all that move in the waters. All birds of the air, glorify the Lord, praise Him and highly exalt Him forever. Glorify the Lord, O beasts of the wild, and all you flocks and herds. O men and women everywhere, glorify the Lord, praise Him and highly exalt Him forever.

Doxology
Let us glorify the Lord: Father, Son, and Holy Spirit. In the firmament of his power, glorify the Lord, praise Him and highly exalt Him forever.

A Song of Praise
Glory to You, Lord God of our fathers; You are worthy of praise; glory to You. Glory to You for the radiance of Your holy Name; we will praise You and highly exalt You forever.

Prayers of Petition
BCP *(adaptation mine)*
Most merciful God, I confess that I have sinned against You in thought, word, and deed, by what I have done, and by what I have left undone. I have not loved You with my whole heart; I have not loved my neighbor as myself. I am truly sorry and I humbly repent. For the sake of Your Son Jesus Christ have mercy on me and forgive me; that I may delight in Your will, and walk in Your ways, to the glory of Your Name. *Amen.*

Almighty God has mercy on me. He forgives me all my sins through our Lord Jesus Christ. He strengthens me in all goodness, and by the power of the Holy Spirit keeps me in eternal life. *Amen.*

Scriptures for the Day

BCP *(adaptation mine)*
Lord, open my lips and my mouth shall proclaim Your praise.

Glory to the Father, and to the Son, and to the Holy Spirit: As it was in the beginning, is now, and will be forever. *Amen.*

The Psalms

Prayerfully read Psalms selected for the day or in sequence.

(At the end of the Psalms)
Glory to the Father, and to the Son, and to the Holy Spirit: As it was in the beginning, is now, and will be forever. Amen.

During a time of silence and listening prayer reflect on the passages you have read.

Old Testament Reading

Systemically read passages from Old Testament books.

(Before the Reading)
Hope in the Word
Psalm 119:73-74, NIV
Your hands made me and formed me; give me understanding to learn your commands. May those who fear you rejoice when they see me, for I have put my hope in your word.

(After the Reading)
The Word of the Lord. Thanks be to God.

During a time of silence and listening prayer reflect on the passages you have read.

New Testament Reading

Systemically read passages from New Testament Books.

(Before the Reading)
Prayer for Spiritual Vision
Ephesians 1:17-19 *(adapted from the NIV)*
O glorious Father, give me the Spirit of wisdom and revelation, so that I may know You better. I pray also that the eyes of my heart may be enlightened in order that I may know the hope to which You have called me, the riches of my glorious inheritance in the saints, and Your incomparably great power for us who believe.

(After the Reading)
The Word of the Lord. Thanks be to God.

During a time of silence and listening prayer reflect on the passages you have read.

Prayers of Petition

The Lord's Prayer
BCP
Our Father in heaven, hallowed be Your Name, your kingdom come, Your will be done, on earth as in heaven. Give us today our daily bread. Forgive us our sins as we forgive those who sin against us. Save us from the time of trial and deliver us from evil. For the kingdom, the power, and the glory are Yours, now and forever. Amen.

For Saturdays
BCP
Almighty God, who after the creation of the world rested from all Your works and sanctified a day of rest for all Your creatures: Grant that we, putting away all earthly anxieties, may be duly prepared for the service of Your sanctuary, and that our rest here upon earth may be a preparation for the eternal rest promised to Your people in heaven; through Jesus Christ our Lord. Amen.

Prayer of Stillness and Trust
Psalm 46:10; Ps 37:1-7 *(adapted from the NIV)*
"Be still and know that I am God; I will be exalted among the nations. I will be exalted in the earth." Don't worry about the wicked. Don't envy those who do wrong. For like grass, they soon fade away. Like springtime flowers, they soon wither.

I will trust in the LORD and do good. Then I will live safely in the land and prosper. I will take delight in the LORD, and He will give me my heart's desires.

I commit everything I do to the LORD. I trust him, and he will help me. He will make my innocence as clear as the dawn, and the justice of my cause will shine like the noonday sun.

Prayer for Freedom and Discipline
Lord Jesus, You have broken the chains.
Philippians 2:13-18 *(adapted from the NKJV)*
Lord Jesus, You have broken the chains. You are at work in me both to will and to act according to Your good purpose. I will not complain. I will

not argue. I will be blameless and pure, a child of God without fault in a crooked and depraved generation. I shine like a star in the black sky. I hold out the Word of Life. I labor for Your reward. Though I am poured out like a drink-offering for the sacrifice and service of Your church, I will be glad and rejoice with Your church. Your church will be glad and rejoice with me. The substance, image and reflection of my life shall be one in the same. And this tree will sprout leaves today.

Promise of Healing
***Jeremiah 30:17*, NLT**
"I will give you back your health and heal your wounds," says the LORD

Promise of Divine Assistance
***Psalm 32:8-10*, NIV**
I will instruct you and teach you in the way you should go; I will counsel you with my loving eye on you. Do not be like the horse or the mule, which have no understanding but must be controlled by bit and bridle or they will not come to you. Many are the woes of the wicked, but the LORD's unfailing love surrounds the one who trusts in him.

Take your personal needs before the Lord through extemporaneous prayer.

Confessions of Faith

The Apostles' Creed
BCP *(adaptation mine)*
I believe in God, the Father almighty, Creator of heaven and earth. I believe in Jesus Christ, His only Son, our Lord. He was conceived by the power of the Holy Spirit and born of the Virgin Mary. He suffered under Pontius Pilate, was crucified, died, and was buried. He descended to the dead. On the third day he rose again. He ascended into heaven and is seated at the right hand of the Father. He will come again to judge the living and the dead. I believe in the Holy Spirit, the holy Christian Church, the communion of saints, the forgiveness of sins, the resurrection of the body, and the life everlasting. Amen.

Confession of Faith in the Father's Care
***Matthew 6:25–33** (adapted from the NLT)*
I do not worry about my clothes. I look at the lilies and how they grow. They don't work or make their clothing, yet Solomon in all his glory was not dressed as beautifully as they are. And if You care so wonderfully for flowers that are here today and gone tomorrow, won't You more surely care for me? I have enough faith to receive Your constant care.

Fruitfulness Confession
***Psalm 52:8–9**, NIV*
…I am like an olive tree flourishing in the house of God; I trust in God's unfailing love for ever and ever. For what you have done I will always praise you in the presence of your faithful people. And I will hope in your name, for your name is good. *Amen.*

Burden Casting Confession
***Psalm 55:22; 1 Peter 5:6–7** (adapted from the NKJV)*
Today, I cast my burden upon You, Lord. You will sustain me. As I stand in the righteousness of Jesus, You will never permit me to be shaken, to slip or to fall. Therefore, I humble myself under Your mighty hand, O God. Exalt me in due time. I cast all my care upon You, for You care for me.

Confession of Mercy and Blessing
***Psalm 90:13–17** (adapted from the NLT)*
Lord Jesus, You come to me in mercy; Your love is my portion today. As this day begins, I feast on Your truth and presence and I will joyfully sing throughout the day and night of Your unfailing love. Give us gladness in proportion to our former misery! Replace the evil years with good. Let us see Your miracles again; let our children see Your glory at work. And Lord, show us Your approval and make our efforts successful. Yes, make our efforts successful!

I Am Not Ashamed
***Romans 1:16–17; 1 Timothy 4:12–16; 2 Timothy 1:12** (adapted from the NKJV)*
I am not ashamed of the gospel, because it is the power of God for the salvation of everyone who believes. For in the gospel a righteousness from

God is revealed, one that is by faith from first to last, just as it is written: *"The righteous will live by faith."*

I will be an example to the believers in word, in conduct, in love, in spirit, in faith, in purity. I will give attention to reading, to exhortation, and to doctrine. I will not neglect God's gifts in me. I will meditate on these things; give myself entirely to them so that my progress may be evident to all. I will be careful that what I say and what I do agree, for in doing this, I will find my own salvation and be a blessing to those who hear me.

I am not ashamed, for I know whom I have believed and am persuaded that He is able to keep what I have committed to Him until that Day.

Benediction

BCP
Lord Jesus Christ, You stretched out Your arms of love on the hard wood of the cross that everyone might come within the reach of Your saving embrace: So clothe us in Your Spirit that we, reaching forth our hands in love, may bring those who do not know You to the knowledge and love of You; for the honor of your Name. Amen.

Ephesians 3:20-21 (adapted from the KJV)
Now unto Him who is able to do exceeding abundantly above all that we ask or think, according to the power at work in us, Unto Him be glory in the church by Christ Jesus throughout all ages, world without end. Amen.

7 DAYS OF PRAYER

Evening Prayer

Call to Worship / Invocation

BCP *(adaptation mine)*
Psalm 141:2
Let my prayer be set forth in Your sight as incense, the lifting up of my hands as the evening sacrifice.

Philippians 1:2
Grace … and peace from God our Father and from the Lord Jesus Christ.

Psalm 96:9
Worship the Lord in the beauty of His holiness; let the whole earth tremble before Him.

Psalm 74:15, 16
Yours is the day, O God, Yours also the night; You established the moon and the sun. You fixed all the boundaries of the earth; You made both summer and winter.

Psalm 16:7, 8
I will bless the Lord who gives me counsel; my heart teaches me, night after night. I have set the Lord always before me; because He is at my right hand, I shall not fall.

Amos 5:8

Seek Him who made the stars and turns deep darkness into the morning, and darkens the day into night, who calls for the waters of the sea and pours them out upon the surface of the earth: The Lord is His name.

John 8:12

Jesus said, *"I am the light of the world; whoever follows me will not walk in darkness but have the light of life."*

Psalm 139:11, 12

If I say, *"Surely the darkness will cover me, and the light around me turn to night,"* darkness is not dark to You, O Lord; the night is as bright as the day; darkness and light to You are both alike.

Prayers of Repentance

1 John 1:9-10, NKJV

If we confess our sins, He is faithful and just to forgive us our sins and to cleanse us from all unrighteousness. If we say that we have not sinned, we make Him a liar, and His word is not in us.

BCP *(adaptation mine)*

Here in Your presence, Almighty God, I bow in silence, and with penitent and obedient heart confess my sins, so that I may obtain forgiveness by Your infinite goodness and mercy. Most merciful God, I confess that I have sinned against You in thought, word, and deed, by what I have done, and by what I have left undone. I have not loved You with my whole heart; I have not loved my neighbor as myself. I am truly sorry and I humbly repent. For the sake of Your Son Jesus Christ have mercy on me and forgive me; that I may delight in Your will, and walk in Your ways, to the glory of Your Name. *Amen.*

Almighty God has mercy on me, He forgives me all my sins through our Lord Jesus Christ. He strengthens me in all goodness, and by the power of the Holy Spirit keeps me in eternal life. *Amen.*

Evening Praise

Choose all or any as needed.

BCP *(adaptation mine)*
Lord, open my lips and my mouth shall proclaim Your praise.

O Gracious Light
BCP
O gracious light, pure brightness of the everliving Father in heaven, O Jesus Christ, holy and blessed! Now as we come to the setting of the sun, and our eyes behold the vesper light, we sing Your praises, O God: Father, Son, and Holy Spirit. You are worthy at all times to be praised by happy voices, O Son of God, O Giver of life, and to be glorified through all the worlds.

Psalm of Rest
Psalm 23, **NIV**
The LORD is my shepherd, I lack nothing. He makes me lie down in green pastures, he leads me beside quiet waters, he refreshes my soul. He guides me along the right paths for his name's sake. Even though I walk through the darkest valley, I will fear no evil, for you are with me; your rod and your staff, they comfort me.

You prepare a table before me in the presence of my enemies. You anoint my head with oil; my cup overflows. Surely your goodness and love will follow me all the days of my life, and I will dwell in the house of the LORD forever.

Exhortation to Rest
Hebrews 4:9–16, **NIV**
There remains, then, a Sabbath-rest for the people of God; for anyone who enters God's rest also rests from their works, just as God did from his. Let us, therefore, make every effort to enter that rest, so that no one will perish by following their example of disobedience.

For the word of God is alive and active. Sharper than any double-edged sword, it penetrates even to dividing soul and spirit, joints and marrow; it judges the thoughts and attitudes of the heart. Nothing in all creation is hidden from God's sight. Everything is uncovered and laid bare before the eyes of him to whom we must give account.

God's Faithfulness at Night
Psalm 92:1–5, **NIV**

It is good to praise the LORD and make music to your name, O Most High, proclaiming your love in the morning and your faithfulness at night, to the music of the ten-stringed lyre and the melody of the harp.

For you make me glad by your deeds, LORD; I sing for joy at what your hands have done. How great are your works, LORD, how profound your thoughts!

Glory to the Father, and to the Son, and to the Holy Spirit: As it was in the beginning, is now, and will be forever. *Amen.*

The Psalms for the Evening

(At the end of the Psalms)
Glory to the Father, and to the Son, and to the Holy Spirit: As it was in the beginning, is now, and will be forever. *Amen.*

During a time of silence and listening prayer reflect on the passages you have read.

Old Testament Reading

(After the Reading)
The Word of the Lord. Thanks be to God.

During a time of silence and listening prayer reflect on the passages you have read.

New Testament Reading

(After the Reading)
The Word of the Lord. Thanks be to God.

During a time of silence and listening prayer reflect on the passages you have read.

Evening Worship

Choose all or any as needed.

The Song of Mary
Luke 1:46–55
BCP
My soul proclaims the greatness of the Lord, my spirit rejoices in God my Savior; for He has looked with favor on His lowly servant. From this day all generations will call me blessed: the Almighty has done great things for me, and holy is His Name. He has mercy on those who fear Him in every generation. He has shown the strength of his arm, He has scattered the proud in their conceit. He has cast down the mighty from their thrones and has lifted up the lowly. He has filled the hungry with good things, and the rich He has sent away empty. He has come to the help of his servant Israel, for He has remembered his promise of mercy, the promise He made to our fathers, to Abraham and His children forever.

Glory to the Father and to the Son, and to the Holy Spirit: as it was in the beginning, is now, and will be forever. *Amen.*

Song of Simeon
Luke 2:29–32
BCP
Lord, You now have set Your servant free to go in peace as You have promised; For these eyes of mine have seen the Savior, whom You have prepared for all the world to see: A Light to enlighten the nations, and the glory of Your people Israel.

Glory to the Father, and to the Son, and to the Holy Spirit: as it was in the beginning, is now, and will be forever. *Amen.*

The Apostles' Creed
BCP *(adaptation mine)*
I believe in God, the Father almighty, creator of heaven and earth. I believe in Jesus Christ, His only son, our Lord. He was conceived by the

power of the Holy Spirit and born of the Virgin Mary. He suffered under Pontius Pilate, was crucified, died, and was buried. He descended to the dead. On the third day He rose again. He ascended into heaven and is seated at the right hand of the Father. He will come again to judge the living and the dead. I believe in the Holy Spirit, the holy Christian Church, the communion of saints, the forgiveness of sins, the resurrection of the body, and the life everlasting. *Amen.*

Prayers of Petition

The Lord's Prayer
BCP
Our Father in heaven, hallowed be Your Name, Your kingdom come, Your will be done, on earth as in heaven. Give us today our daily bread. Forgive us our sins as we forgive those who sin against us. Save us from the time of trial and deliver us from evil. For the kingdom, the power, and the glory are Yours, now and forever. Amen

Take your personal needs before the Lord.

Evening Prayers As Needed

BCP *(adaptation mine)*
That this evening may be holy, good, and peaceful, That Your holy angels may lead us in paths of peace and goodwill, that we may rest in Your grace, our sins and offenses, forgiven. That there may be peace to Your Church and to the whole world.

Against Perils
BCP
Be our light in the darkness, O Lord, and in Your great mercy defend us from all perils and dangers of this night, for the love of Your only Son, our Savior Jesus Christ. *Amen.*

For Protection
BCP
O God, the life of all who live, the light of the faithful, the strength of those who labor, and the repose of the dead: We thank You for the blessings of the day that is past, and humbly ask for Your protection through the coming night. Bring us in safety to the morning hours; through Him who died and rose again for us, Your Son our Savior Jesus Christ. *Amen.*

For the Presence of Christ
BCP
Lord Jesus, stay with us, for evening is at hand and the day is past; be our companion in the way, kindle our hearts, and awaken hope, that we may know You as you are revealed in Scripture and the breaking of bread. Grant this for the sake of Your love. *Amen.*

For Rest
BCP
Keep watch, dear Lord, with those who work, or watch, or weep this night, and give Your angels charge over those who sleep. Tend the sick, Lord Christ; give rest to the weary, bless the dying, soothe the suffering, pity the afflicted, shield the joyous; and all for Your love's sake. *Amen.*

The General Thanksgiving
BCP
Almighty God, Father of all mercies, we Your unworthy servants give You humble thanks for all your goodness and loving-kindness to us and to all whom you have made. We bless You for our creation, preservation, and all the blessings of this life; but above all for Your immeasurable love in the redemption of the world by our Lord Jesus Christ; for the means of grace, and for the hope of glory. And, we pray, give us such an awareness of Your mercies, That with truly thankful hearts we may show forth Your praise, not only with our lips, but in our lives, by giving up ourselves to Your service, and by walking before You in holiness and righteousness all our days; through Jesus Christ our Lord, to whom, with You and the Holy Spirit, be honor and glory throughout all ages. *Amen.*

Be Still, and Know
Psalm 46:10; Ps 37:1–7 *(adapted from the NIV)*
"Be still and know that I am God; I will be exalted among the nations. I will be exalted in the earth." Don't worry about the wicked. Don't envy those who do wrong. For like grass, they soon fade away. Like springtime flowers, they soon wither.

I will trust in the LORD and do good. Then I will live safely in the land and prosper. I will take delight in the LORD, and He will give me my heart's desires.

I commit everything I do to the LORD. I trust him, and he will help me. He will make my innocence as clear as the dawn, and the justice of my cause will shine like the noonday sun.

Benediction

For Peace
BCP
Eternal God, in whose perfect kingdom no sword is drawn but the sword of righteousness, no strength known but the strength of love: So mightily spread abroad Your Spirit, that all peoples may be gathered under the banner of the Prince of Peace, as children of one Father; to whom be dominion and glory, now and forever. *Amen.*

For these and all his mercies, God's holy Name be blessed and praised; through Jesus Christ our Lord. *Amen.*

MEET THE AUTHOR

Dr. Stephen Phifer

A third-generation minister with the Assemblies of God, Stephen Phifer serves the Lord as writer, musician, teacher, and all-around encourager. With more than 50 years of ministry on his record, he remains active in music education and worship arts education. He holds bachelors and masters degrees in music education and a doctorate in worship studies. This is his sixth book to reach print, and more are on the way. He is married to a wonderful musician and music educator, Freeda. In 2024, they celebrated 50 years of a powerful and peaceful partnership. Find more of Steve's writing at www.StevePhifer.com.

www.ingramcontent.com/pod-product-compliance
Lightning Source LLC
Chambersburg PA
CBHW072213070526
44585CB00015B/1313